I0152895

Eleven Great Religions
of the World Today

Eleven Great Religions
of the World Today

A Quick Description

HAP C. S. LYDA

RESOURCE *Publications* · Eugene, Oregon

ELEVEN GREAT RELIGIONS OF THE WORLD TODAY
A Quick Description

Copyright © 2020 Hap C. S. Lyda. All rights reserved. Except for brief quotations in critical publications or reviews, no part of this book may be reproduced in any manner without prior written permission from the publisher. Write: Permissions, Wipf and Stock Publishers, 199 W. 8th Ave., Suite 3, Eugene, OR 97401.

Resource Publications
An Imprint of Wipf and Stock Publishers
199 W. 8th Ave., Suite 3
Eugene, OR 97401

www.wipfandstock.com

PAPERBACK ISBN: 978-1-7252-8505-7
HARDCOVER ISBN: 978-1-7252-8506-4
EBOOK ISBN: 978-1-7252-8507-1

Manufactured in the U.S.A.   11/06/20

Contents

Introduction

WHY THIS BOOK

This book is a brief, simplified presentation of eleven major world religions from their beginnings to the present. These eleven major religions are active in the world today. These eleven have been chosen from countless religions. The two criteria for choosing these are largest size and/or largest influence.

In order to study these religions it is not necessary that you be a member of any one of them, or of any religion. If you happen to select membership in one of these as a result of your study that is your decision, for this book is not intended to be a missionary device to convert you. This book is intended to enrich your days on planet Earth with knowledge of the largest phenomenon in the world—religion.

The eleven selected religions claim five billion members out of the seven billion people on Earth. Five billion is huge when compared to any one nation; for example, the United States of America has a population of less than four hundred million, which is less than ten percent of the aggregate eleven religions.

Yesteryear these eleven major religions were located over there somewhere in some foreign country. If you are like most people, you have grown up in a family or culture wherein one of these eleven religions was dominant. If so, then ten of these religions may seem strange to you. In your lifetime the world society has gotten smaller in the way that the most remote religion may now be a factor in your community or business or travel. Yesteryear Christianity was predominant where I lived in the United States; now my next-door neighbors are Hindus, down the road live members of Judaism, not five miles away is a Buddhist temple, across town is a Sikh sanctuary, and I could go on in such manner for the rest of the eleven religions. Only a few years ago most of these religions other than one's own were alien. Now all eleven are present nearly wherever we live.

A surprise to some people is that other religions rather than their own are just as significant to those who hold them as is their own to themselves. All eleven of the religions described in this book give their adherents sustaining beliefs about the fundamentals: origin, meaning, and destiny of life. Jain members are quite confident their religion answers these fundamentals, as are Taoists or Buddhists or Baha'is. Members of these religions do not yearn to become members of some other religion in order to find answers to the fundamentals of life. They have their own answers.

One of the chief characteristics of these religions is the creation of a society of persons who live in similar ways. In other words, these religions create unique cultures. Religions of the Middle East—Hinduism, Buddhism, Jainism, and Sikhism—create a way of living that is identifiable. So do the religions in the Far East—Taoism, Confucianism, and Shintoism—create a life mode for their constituents. In similar manner so do the religions of the Near East—Judaism, Christianity, Islam, and Baha'i—create a civil manner for their adherents.

VALUES OF RELIGION

The values of religion may be overlooked in a world of so many activities and attractions. Even members may participate in a religion minimally without realizing religion's great values. One is *community*. Community offers fulfillment of what is generally viewed as an essential human need—belonging. Belonging fulfills our social need. All eleven of the great religions treated in this book furnish the value of community. Members are cordial to one another. They shake hands or hug or at least smile. Being together is as old as Adam and Eve, or Rama and Sita. Christianity began with a grouping of three thousand in community.

A second value of religion is *conduct*. Closely associated with community is conduct. All of these eleven religions have codes of conduct. Codes of conduct, variously called ethics, morals, mores, or folkways, are advocated by them. Many a conversation has considered the question of where we would get our proper ways of behavior were it not for religions? The answer may be nowhere else. Ethical conduct takes community deeper; it delves into survival of the species. Some of the rules may be rather petty, such as how far one may travel on a holy day to get to a place of worship, but others have to do with survival itself, such as you shall not kill one another. All eleven of the great religions treated in this book stress the value of conduct.

A third value of religion is *care*. Care is the giving of assistance when someone is in need. Religions give solace to the grieving. Religions garner food for the needy. Religions offer consolation to the imprisoned. Religions provide comfort to the destitute. Religions bestow nurture for the orphaned. The anecdote is told of an early Judaism scholar who, when asked what was basic in his religion replied that all teaching could be uttered while he stood on one foot: his answer was "love." A word used by ethicists in our time for love is caring.

A fourth all-encompassing value of religion is *culture*. Culture is "the way we do things around here." It is the local way of life that defines us. It includes the many aspects of daily living. It fulfills our need for community. It directs human conduct. It imparts care as needed. It casts an aura of sacredness on festivals and worship. It furnishes the robe of survival with its several panels of faith, hope, and love. It addresses our insatiable curiosity about the mysteries of life and afterlife. Culture is the whole of living. I have a colleague who says that he is an "agnostic Christian." He defines that as one who cannot prove the divinity of Jesus, or the resurrection from the dead, or the housing of heaven, or even the existence of a personal god; but he likes the culture Christianity creates. The great religions treated in this book create vital cultures.

TABLE OF CONTENTS

In very general terms the Middle East religions have fostered an attitude of living which could be simplified as "escape" from earthly life. The Far East religions have fashioned a way that could be summarized as "enjoy" earthly life. The Near East religions have formed a model of "endure" earthly life. These three modes, escape, enjoy, and endure, compose the three sections of this book.

Each section is divided according to the religions that arose in its respective geographical area. Thus, the table of contents is:

ADHERENTS WORLDWIDE

Note that the numbering of adherents in any of the religions is inexact. The numbers vary according to how active the participants are.

The following figures are compiled from a variety of sources, basically from the *New York Times Almanac*. Shintoism is particularly problematic in that historically it included all the population of Japan. Some counters today put Shinto membership at four million who actively advocate or participate in public ways, but the current one hundred twenty seven million citizens of Japan probably all have some cultural connection to Shintoism.

- Hinduism: One billion.
- Jainism: Four million.
- Buddhism: Five hundred million.
- Sikhism: Thirty million.
- Taoism: Fifty million.
- Confucianism: Six million.
- Shintoism: Four million / one hundred twenty-seven million.
- Judaism: Seventeen million.
- Christianity: Two billion, three hundred million.
- Islam: One billion, six hundred million.
- Baha'i: Seven million.

SECTION I

Middle East: Escape

Section I describes the Middle East religions of Hinduism, Jainism, Buddhism, and Sikhism. These religions arose in India and/or its adjoining territories. They continue to have their largest memberships there. Hinduism is the collective name for the indigenous religions from the earliest time in this geographical area. There were, and still are, many cultural areas with local religion practices in India. The areas may have different rituals or myths, but they have common basic elements of religion. In general the native religions, with some features added by successive invaders, were coalesced under the title of "Hinduism." The name Hinduism quite probably was coined by invading powers ages ago who considered themselves superior to the natives; the invaders called all who lived beside and east of the Indus River, "Indus—Hindus." The waves of invaders were many, notably Aryan, Mongol, Muslim, and British.

The pervading feature of the four Middle East religions is "escape," escape from earthly life to absorption into Ultimate Reality / Brahman. Doctrines were formed millennia ago that seek a destiny of total removal from common life. The ways to escape vary between the four Middle East religions, but escape is a demanding theme of them all. A common belief is reincarnation, which gives a person more chances than one to exit life and be absorbed into Brahman. In other words, escape to non-earthly being is life's intended destiny.

1

Hinduism

HINDUISM IS A BLEND of ancient religions of India based on good works that enable a person to escape from unsatisfactory human life to absorption into Brahman.

Hinduism, taken as a whole, is the oldest of the Middle East religions. It is often called "The Eternal Way." The singular title of Hinduism probably was first given by the Aryans who came from the west and invaded India sometime near 1500 BCE. They blended their cultural ways with the native ways. A major contribution of the Aryans was the formation of literature that became sacred scripture for Hinduism, the *Vedas*.

The *Vedas* are believed to have been directly revealed by the gods to seers among the Aryans. The *Vedas* are composed of four books: *Rig Veda*, *Sama Veda*, *Yajur Veda*, and *Atharva Veda*. The term *Veda* means wisdom or knowledge. The *Vedas* contain hymns, mantras, philosophy, ethics, and guidance for the religion leaders for performing rituals.

The *Rig Veda* is composed of one thousand twenty-eight hymns. These mention many primitive gods, in particular Indra, Agni, Varuna, and Soma. Indra is the god-in-charge. Indra is lauded as the god who raises the sun, flings bolts at enemies, and rules the ways of humans. Agni is the god of fire, all fires, including lightning, sun, and hearth. Agni is praised for dispelling the night, being easy to approach, and bestowing well-being upon humans. Varuna is often mentioned as the god of the sky, sea, and land, as well as being the instigator of the cosmic formation. Varuna is honored for releasing persons from bondage, and giving renewed and long life. Soma has a mixed identity, sometimes as a god and sometimes as a hallucinogenic plant used especially by the priestly class. As time has progressed many other gods have received accolades for their particular roles that keep the universe working.

Finally a super force beyond any god is described and identified as Brahman or Brahman-atman. Brahman is the overreaching spiritual dimension of all that exists. Brahman is the force, not a god. Brahman is both no thing and all. Brahman has no anthropomorphic being. Brahman has no gender. Brahman has no responsibilities. Brahman is the amorphous, ultimate, non-spatial being-ness. Brahman might be compared very loosely to the internet "Cloud" in our contemporary world. Brahman is both the source and the end-goal in Hinduism. The meaning of life is to escape earthly existence (samsara) and be absorbed into Brahman (moksha). When Brahman is spoken of as Brahman-atman it means that the soul-essence of a person, called atman, has escaped existence and is united with Brahman. Absorption into Brahman is the hoped-for destiny for human beings. When the soul-essence of a person is absorbed into Brahman the person will never be born again, will remain within the all-ness of Brahman forever. Once a soul has escaped earthly, material being, it is never reborn/reincarnated.

Over the course of centuries further Hindu holy literature beyond the *Vedas* was written, notably the *Upanishads*. These are profound discourses in the interpretation of Hinduism. In addition mythological writings were composed which are still highly popular today. One is the *Bhagavad Gita*, a mythical story of military combat that probes human ethics to its very deepest interior. Another popular mythical story is *Ramayana*. It is contained in a larger work, called the *Mahabharata*, in which the monkey god, Hanuman, comes to the aid of Rama to rescue his wife, Sita, from the demon god Ravana.

By our time, a Trimurti/trinity of other gods receive special reverence in Hinduism for the roles they play in human life: Brahma the creator, Vishnu the preserver, and Shiva the destroyer. Furthermore, these male gods have taken wives who are revered as divinities. Still furthermore, there are countless other gods who are worshipped in various localities. Observe that many gods are no problem in Hinduism, because all of them point to Brahman; the adherents know all gods are temporary, even as all humans are temporary, even all the universe is temporary. The goal of Hinduism religion is to escape earthly transiency (samsara), and be absorbed into the permanency (moksha) of Brahman.

One important doctrine of Hinduism is varna, the caste system. Probably caste originated as a power play by the priests and rulers following 1500 BCE. They viewed themselves as being at the top of humanity. Over time many lower castes were created to hem people into various professions and labors. Today varna has been outlawed in civil matters in India, but remains spottily observed in popular conduct.

Another important doctrine is reincarnation. A person's life begins with an incarnation. The Brahman/Oversoul becomes a baby, a human. Human life is not ideal. Human life has to struggle to live. Human life may have inadequate shelter or insufficient food or debilitating diseases. The ultimate meaning of life is for one's essence/atman to escape its struggles and sufferings. Human destiny is for one's soul to be reabsorbed into the Brahman essence from which it came.

Escape from the banes of life is via dis-incarnating back into Brahman. If a person does not reach moksha the first time around, a person gets a second chance through being reincarnated; and another chance, *ad infinitum*, until a person unites with the force (Brahman) which gives existence in the first place. The origin of life is a mystery, but life happens. Doctrinally, life comes from the ultimate source of all existence, Brahman. Escaping earthly/material existence back into Brahman is the intendedness for humans.

Whether or not a person attains moksha is decided by karma. Karma is the actions of a person during life that are good or evil; they determine whether a person moves up or down in the scale of varna/caste. A person's destiny is not judged by a personal god, by any divinity; nor by sin or grace; only by karma, which is as constant as a computer.

A large variety of rituals have been developed in the many localities of the Middle East to speed adherents to Brahman. Cleansing in water is important before worshipping. A type of ritual similar to Holy Communion, called Tulci, is practiced by some, featuring a flame rather than wine or wafer. Use of yogas, mantras, prayer wheels, celebrations, rebuilding statues of the gods, and the like are directed by the priestly class for the speeding of persons to moksha.

As a general observation, nearly anything virtuous may be incorporated into Hinduism, be they gods or rituals or meditations or plaster images, since all point to Brahman. Nearly any mode of worship/puja has efficacy if it directs a person to the ultimate condition of Brahman-atman.

There are many sites that are revered by Hindus. One of the most popular is the Ganges River in India. The River provides all the blessings water has to give, especially cleansing of the soul and blessings for living. It bestows merit on persons who die at the River. It gives blessing to the ashen remains of Hindus who are cremated on the banks of the River.

The official places of Hindu worship are called mandirs, shrines, and temples. Some of the usual terms for official leaders are brahmin, guru, mahant, pandit, rishi, swami, sadhu, and yogi.

Some holidays are universally observed, notably the spring festival of Holi, the fall festival of Dasehra, and the New Year festival of Divali. Many holidays and festivals are observed according to geographical areas.

Hinduism has about six thousand years of history. It has survived changes of civil governments, foreign military invasions, alien cultural influences, competing religions, civil discontent, coming and going of many divinities, changing leadership by the Brahmin priestly professionals, and new sacred literature composed by remarkable authors and/or inspired by the gods. It has been expanded by charismatic gurus. It absorbs every facet of life namable. It thrives on multiplicity, rather than on singular orthodoxy or orthopraxy.

Anything, any god, human or mythically divine, can be worked into Hinduism since it points to Brahman.

Adherents of the many types of Hinduism added together number approximately one billion, making it the third largest of our eleven religions. For these billion, Hinduism is the immovable rock of belief about origin, meaning, and destiny of life. Hinduism's largest concentration of adherents is in its home of India. During the last one hundred fifty years Hinduism has spread into nearly all countries of the world.

Hinduism is the primal religion of the Middle East, the collage-like parent with the goal of finally escaping earthly existence and being absorbed into the supreme force of the cosmos, Brahman.

2

Jainism

Jainism is a reformation of Hinduism doctrines on how to overcome the banes of the body and attain the victory of soul-union with the ultimate force, Brahman.

Jainism is the second in order of time for Middle East religions. The word Jain is translated into English as "overcomer" or "victor."

Jainism arose in western India in the sixth century BCE. At first the religion was a contender with orthodox Hinduism, trying to improve Hinduism. In the course of history, Hinduism largely has absorbed Jainism. Figures of membership in the early centuries are not forthcoming. The total of Jains presently is counted as slightly over four million. Today nearly all Jains live in India, although a noteworthy cadre have immigrated to Great Britain, and smaller chapters are scattered throughout the Western world.

Credit for founding the religion of Jainism is given to Nataputta Vardhamana. At about age forty he began publicly protesting certain aspects of Hinduism. When he became respected as the leader of the protests he was given the title of Mahavira (Great Hero). In a way he is not considered the original Jainist, inasmuch as Jain doctrine asserts religion truth has been revealed, then departed therefrom, many times since the beginning of human existence. Historically he is viewed as the founder of the religion of Jainism.

The dates for the life of Nataputta usually given are 599–527 BCE. His family were members of the next to the highest caste in India, Kshatriya. Their home was in the city of Valsali in the region of Magadah, India. The family was wealthy, but Nataputta was not satisfied with luxury. When Hindu ascetics passed by the house one day, Nataputta was intrigued. After his parents died, he joined this ascetic mode of Hinduism.

At about age forty he declared himself free from all things material and all human ties. He declared his soul free from all the cycles of reincarnation. He went about India for the next thirty years teaching his way of life to others. His teaching drew heavily on Hinduism, and yet was reformative enough to be the beginning of the Jain religion.

Jainism reinterprets the basic Hinduism doctrines of reincarnation, karma, caste, asceticism, ahimsa, divinity, and sacred scripture so that believers may be absorbed better into the ultimate force of life, Brahman.

From Hinduism, Mahavira Nataputta kept reincarnation as the hoped-for upward path to Brahman, but reformed it. Hinduism based reincarnation on a kind of cosmic report card; whether a person was reborn into a higher or lower caste or subcaste depended on the metaphysical scheme of karma action which is beyond human understanding. Hinduism defined karma in terms of works. If the good works outweighed the evil works, then a soul moved up the ladder of caste through the levels of reincarnation toward Brahman.

Freeing the soul from the mathematics of karma is the goal of Jainism. Mahavira Nataputta changed the nature of karma from the mystical and mysterious virtue grading to particles of matter that fasten themselves mystically to the soul. The amount of material clinging to a soul determines the caste rebirth. These particles of matter are detriments to true life. It is possible to rid oneself of karma particles by practicing the Three Gems / Ratna-Kraya of correct faith, correct knowledge, and correct conduct. Specific mores for the devoted disciples are the five commandments of nonviolence/

ahimsa (no harm to living things), truthfulness, non-stealing, celibacy, and non-possession. Other lists of the correct practices state them as no acquiring of material objects, no lying, no stealing, and sexual restraint. Jainism idealizes celibacy, and requires an unmarital status for monks and nuns.

From Hinduism, Mahavira Nataputta kept the varna/caste system, but declared that a person in any caste could reach enlightenment, not just the highest class. Anyone from any caste could escape unsatisfactory life on Earth and achieve moksha. He added that women as surely as men could reach enlightenment.

From Hinduism, Mahavira Nataputta kept asceticism, but he magnified it. Giving up, doing without, and eating no meat, killing no life, and deep meditation are ideal modes of constant, consistent conduct to bring a person into the fulfillment of life. Mahavira Nataputta wore no clothing, summer or winter. It is told that critics once built a fire under him to test his rejection of being comfortable with the accoutrements of material life, but he allowed himself to be scorched rather than admit the material accident of pain.

From Hinduism, Mahavira Nataputta kept the doctrine of ahimsa, but expanded it. He insisted since all living things, both animals and plants, were sacred products of the handiwork of divinity, no life should be destroyed by human hands. He refrained from stepping on insects. He strained his drinking water to keep from harming even the tiniest bugs that might have gotten into it. He killed no life. He revered planet Earth in all respects. He advocated and observed a vegetarian diet; but not just any vegetables; no root vegetables, because their bulbs contained the seed of life.

From Hinduism, Mahavira Nataputta kept belief in the traditional gods, but considered them to be part of the natural universe rather than stand-apart actors. He taught that none of the gods assisted humans with the living of life. He believed the highest human destiny is to be absorbed back into the mystical, beyond divinity, Brahman; he kept the Hindu term for absorption, moksha. Moksha is to be reached by humans without any assistance from the gods or divinities. Enlightenment must be found on one's own. There is no savior to compensate for wrong doing. Jainism is a self-help way of life. If a person practices the three self-help principles of right faith, right knowledge, and right conduct, enlightenment will follow.

From Hinduism, Mahavira Nataputta kept the sacred literature of the *Vedas*, but he and succeeding Jains wrote additional sacred literature, the *Agamas*. The *Agamas* superseded the *Vedas* of Hinduism. The *Agamas* praise all types of things, nature, souls, and persons. They guide members into the fullness of truth, doctrine, and goodness. Passages extol wisdom, non-injury, asceticism, and enlightenment. A rule for personal conduct is "one who knows what is bad for himself knows what is bad for others."

A unique doctrine of Jainism is there were eras of true religion in the past. They were led by Tirthankaras (ford builders). Jain literature counts twenty-four such persons. The Tirthankaras have crossed over (forded) from material existence into the state of total release (moksha/kevalgyan*)* from this life and from all matter. The Tirthankaras are the saintly ones who show members the way to cross over into enlightenment.

After four hundred years of unity in Jainism, about the year 80 BCE, Jainism divided into the two major sects still active today, the Digambara (sky robed) and the Svetambara (white robed). Digambara Jains are conservative, literalistic, recommend nudity, declare that women cannot achieve soul release, and teach that women are great temptations to men, especially to monks. Digambara denies that Mahavira Nataputta married or had children. Members of this sect may eat only one meal a day donated by a single household.

Svetambara Jains allow men to wear clothing, allow women to participate in all phases of Jainism, and allow eating more than once a day and from more than one household. Furthermore, Svetambaras claim that the nineteenth Tirthankara was a woman. Svetambaras allow monks to keep fourteen possessions, whereas Digambara monks may keep only three. Svetambaras acknowledge the family life of Mahavira Nataputta: wife and one daughter.

Jains have built beautiful temples for pilgrimage and worship. At Palatana, Gujarat, India, the massive Statrunjaya Hill Temple is strikingly unique in its beautiful architecture. In the same city are eight hundred sixty three additional temples. Worship propels persons out of the material, and releases them into kevalgyan (enlightenment).

Jainism observes many festivals. Mahavira Nataputta's birth is celebrated in April. Divali is celebrated in November; it remembers the liberation of Mahavira Nataputta from material things by the lighting of lamps. Paijusana is celebrated in August or September for eight days; it starts the New Year with resolutions for adhering more faithfully to the ways of Jainism; the laity are encouraged to live as monks for at least a day; alms are given to the poor; and a procession honoring the Tirthankaras is paraded on the streets. Kartik Purnima is celebrated in October/November; it is a time of making pilgrimages to sacred Jain sites. Mauna Agyaras is celebrated in November/December; fasting and silent meditation are featured. Annual festivals celebrate the five important events of the Tirthankaras: womb, birth, renunciation, knowledge, and escape from earthly life.

Jainism teaches that the enlightened person understands how karma affects all aspects of life: earth, water, fire, humans, animals, and wind. The enlightened person understands that one's soul-part (atman) is ultimately destined to escape all the hindrances of matter and the self. Jainism doctrine asserts human origin is from the plenteous Brahman, human meaning is escape from burdensome earthly life, and human destiny is final absorption back into Brahman.

3

Buddhism

BUDDHISM SEEKS THE ENLIGHTENMENT realization that all matter, all things, including persons and souls, are illusory.

Buddhism originated in the Middle East about the same time as Jainism in the sixth century BCE. Like Jainism, Buddhism was a reformation movement within Hinduism. Buddhism began with just one person, Siddhartha Gautama, and has grown today to nearly a half billion members. Buddhism was not welcomed by Hinduism and thus moved early to nearby countries. Today it has spread to nearly all regions of the world. Its size makes it the fourth largest of the great religions of the world.

Siddhartha was a nobleman brought up in palace luxury. His father was King Suddhodana of Kapilavatthu, an ancient locality in Majjhimadesa (Middle Country) of India. Kapilavatthu was known as a pleasant kingdom, surrounded by seven very high walls.

Siddhartha's birth story has a miraculous feature. His parents, King Suddhodana and Queen Maya, hoped for a boy child for many years. Queen Maya one night dreamed that a white elephant circled her several times, then entered her side with his trunk and she became pregnant. She delivered Siddhartha successfully, but died within a few days. The King immediately married her sister, Prajapati, who then became the stepmother of Siddhartha.

When Siddhartha was born to King Suddhodana and Queen Maya, Hindu seers pronounced that he was so extraordinary he would become either a great king of all India or a great leader of religion. His father hoped Siddhartha would succeed him and become the great king. The King had Siddhartha educated in all the ways of a prince. Siddhartha became especially adept in the martial arts of the time. The King had Siddhartha marry his cousin, Princess Deyaa/Yasodhara. She and Siddhartha parented a son, Rahula.

When Siddhartha was about thirty years old he chanced about the kingdom and noticed how non-royalty lived. What he saw was not pretty. His ventures to the outer world were summed up in later literature in this way. He saw for the first time a diseased person. He saw for the first time a decrepit person. He saw for the first time a dead person. He was dismayed inasmuch as he had never seen these three *d's* during his palace years.

His agitation over discovering how most people suffered in life led him to seek the cause of disease, decrepitude, and death. These three *d's* he deemed to be the occasions of human suffering and unhappiness. On a fourth journey about town he saw a meditating monk who was perfectly at peace even though surrounded by the three *d's*. Siddhartha was so motivated by the peaceful demeanor of the monk that one night he kissed his wife and son goodbye and stealthily fled the palace to take up the monk's style of life. He mounted his horse, which jumped over the seventy-foot-high city wall, and he rode away to a settlement of monks. He thought surely among them he would find the cure for the unsatisfactoriness the three *d's* dealt common life.

He followed the daily lifestyle of the monks, that of an ascetic. As a monk he lived in isolation from society, except for other ascetics. He studied the words and ways of the gurus who practiced asceticism. He gave up so much food that it is said he survived on only one grain of rice a day. He became so emaciated that the rumor was you could touch his spine by touching his belly button. Some onlookers thought he was actually a sitting corpse.

After several years of trying to be better than even the best ascetic monk he found no answer to the unsatisfactoriness of human life. He gave up his extreme mode of asceticism. He vowed to think on the problem of escape from unsatisfactory life until he found the cause. He told his fellow ascetics he was going to meditate until he understood the answer to the human predicament. He went to a park in the city of Lumbini, just over the boundary of India, in Nepal. He sat under a bodhi tree and thought.

It is told he meditated forty days and forty nights seeking enlightenment. He began by noting earthly life itself is the locale of the three *d*'s. Life is beset with these woes. Then he traced the woes to human wanting, wanting more than life could ever give. Siddhartha posited that the wanting was for the accumulation of illusory lifestyles and abundance of possessions which satisfied naught. He hit upon the depths of wanting with the term "desire." Desire was the bane of existence. Desire was the urge to get and get and get; yet when all of the getting was done, the three *d*'s still haunted life, making living unsatisfactory. He concluded that all life was unsatisfactory, even human life itself. Nevertheless, suicide was not the answer. Persons must go on living. The answer was not physical withdrawal, but mental escape, escape from the mental yearning for things, escape from seeking even wealth, health, and happiness. He centered on the attitude of desire as life's impediment. Desire drove persons to earthly lifelong unsatisfactoriness. Escape from desire was his answer. He came to this mental "enlightenment" during his meditation under the bodhi tree.

Siddhartha then made a daring assertion that the Hindu teaching of the permanency of the soul was a false faith. What Hinduism calls the soul is nothing more than a concatenation of daily activities. The soul as a reality in itself is a mental mistake, an ego delusion, a mythical chimera, nothing. The soul is one more terrestrial entity with no final reality. Like all earthly things, the soul is impermanent. Then he made the crowning heretical assertion: the soul does not exist. This teaching tore the center out of his native Hinduism.

Siddhartha's memorable enlightenment was summed up in his "Four Noble Truths":

1. To live is to suffer.
2. Suffering is caused by desire.

3. Stop desire.
4. Follow the Eightfold Path:
   - Right view, seeing things for what they are.
   - Right intention, determining to follow the Buddha's way.
   - Right speech, not abusing other people, not lying, not chattering idly.
   - Right action, no killing, no stealing, no liquor, no sexual misconduct.
   - Right livelihood, making a living that serves others.
   - Right effort, striving to cultivate virtues that benefit one-self and others.
   - Right mindfulness, focusing on the inner workings of mind and body.
   - Right concentrating on proper meditation.

Through practice of the Four Noble Truths and the Eightfold Path of life a person can reach the awareness that all things, including the soul, are impermanent, not "really" real. At this point of enlightenment, one enters Nirvana.

The life dates of Siddhartha are imprecise, but generally given as 560–480 BCE. He left home at age thirty, and spent about seven years as an ascetic. He was about thirty-seven when he had his en-lightenment under the bodhi tree. He worked the next forty years as the itinerate leader of the way of life he conceived. He welcomed the title of Buddha, the "fully enlightened one." His first followers were the half dozen monks who had been his companions during his ascetic days. The company of followers increased rapidly. One estimate is that within a short time he returned to his father's realm with a company of twenty thousand monks. His father and his step mother became converts from Hinduism. Although Buddha Siddhartha's culture promoted the gender superiority of males, he taught that women could reach enlightenment; he formed an order of nuns for his women followers.

Buddha Siddhartha's disciples formulated a creedal statement as the entry into Buddhism: "I believe in the Buddha, in the Dhar-ma (teachings of the Buddha), and in the Sangha (order of monks)." This Trinitarian Creed is also called the Three Jewels. This creed held Buddhism tightly together until the General Council in 250 BCE. At that time the religion divided into two types, the original, called Theravada, and the variety called Mahayana.

Mahayana adds a belief that has made it the larger of the two types: savior figures. Mahayana adds the teaching that lay people can get help from savior-types called Bodhisattvas. Bodhisattvas are ones who have been successful in reaching enlightenment, but instead of going into isolated Nirvana and forsaking the rest of humanity, they remain connected to society to assist others to reach enlightenment. Today a Mahayanist worship service in Honolulu, Hawaii, United States of America, may look quite like a Christian Protestant Methodist worship service, except with a savior addressed as Buddha/Bodhisattva, rather than Christ Jesus.

By the eighth century CE a third style of Buddhism developed in Tibet, Vajrayana. Vajrayana is basically Buddhist, but is distinct in a few ways, such as placing great emphasis on adherents becoming monks or nuns. A unique practice is the use of prayer wheels to propel followers to enlightenment. In time, the head monk led not only the religion in Tibet, but also Tibet's government, with the title Dalai Lama. Vajrayana recently has been decimated by the government of the People's Republic of China, but continues in spite of persecution. All three types of Buddhism have fostered their own subunits of schools of theology and rituals of practice.

Buddhism is what religion scholars characterize as a universalizing religion, one that seeks to convert the whole world to itself. It does so with the confidence that it has the truth about human origin, meaning, and destiny.

Buddha Siddhartha's interpretation of religion for the Indian subcontinent was revolutionary. It was too revolutionary to be accepted by its parent, Hinduism. While at first Buddha Siddhartha attracted many converts from Hinduism, finally Buddhism had to leave its home because of the entrenchment of Hinduism. Although Buddhism arose at the same time as did Jainism, both of them reform movements, the two religions were too disparate to present a united-front replacement of their parent Hinduism.

Buddhists of all styles observe several festivals. They celebrate Songkran / New Year, in April, emphasizing fun and fellowship, cleaning and cleansing, offerings, and rededication to the Buddhist way of life. Buddhists celebrate Wesak, the birthday of Siddhartha in April or May, with flowers, washing of statues of the Buddha, children dressing up as the Buddha, and noisy firecrackers. Another celebration is Ullambana, in July or August, a release of the spirits of the dead to wander the Earth and receive blessings of comfort. A fourth is the Robe Offering in November, observing a very important sending out of missionaries by the third-century BCE emperor of India, Asoka; it features feasting giving of new robes to monks, and commemorates the night Siddhartha renounced worldly life, and his stepmother, in a single night, spun and wove for Siddhartha his first mendicant's robe, the Great Robe / Mahakathina.

The official leaders of Buddhism are variously called arhat, bodhisattva, clergyman, clergywoman, and lama.

The places of worship are called by several names, such as hut, shrine, stupa, pagoda, vihara, and temple. The entire worship compound is entitled wat.

The sacred scripture gathered by Buddhist scholars is the *Tripitaka*. Scholars in all three of the groups of Buddhists have added other works, some of which have become virtual sacred scriptures, such as Mahayana adding *Sutras* and Vajrayana adding *The Book of the Dead*.

Buddha Siddhartha is said to have given this escape myth to his listeners as a description of his way. Imagine taking a trip across a stream. You get in a boat, push off from the shore, cross the stream, debark on the far shore, and then look back. What you see is no starting shore, no boat, no river, no near shore, and looking at yourself—no person. All is illusion, impermanence.

Buddhism is the enlightenment way of total escape.

4

Sikhism

SIKHISM TEACHES THAT EACH person alone is responsible for increasingly good conduct until the person's soul is reunited with God.

Sikhism was begun about the year 1500 CE. It was composed of elements from Hinduism and Islam, plus the original doctrines of its founder, Nanak.

Nanak was born in Punjab, Pakistan, on November 29, 1469. His parents were merchants. They noted his propensity for things spiritual by the time he was a half dozen years old. When he was a teenager he went to live with his sister's family. He maintained a noticeable spiritual bent, as well as a concern for the welfare of people in general. He married Mata Sulakkhani and fathered two sons; his oldest son, Sri Chand, would become a leader in Sikhism, founding the Udasi School of the religion.

Nanak grew up as a practicing Hindu. He became acquainted with Islam through Muslim expansion in the Punjab. He brought together key elements from both religions. From both he adopted belief in the soul. From Hinduism he taught the orthodoxy of a continuing soul in the process of reincarnation until it was absorbed into abstract Brahman. From Islam he averred that the ultimate divinity was personal, singular, and communicable, with the names God and Allah meaning the one and same divinity.

When Nanak was twenty-seven years old he began traveling and teaching. There are many stories about his work, the historicity of them moot. What is factual is he was very effective in spreading his teaching and making disciples. He was accorded the title of Guru, and when he died, the successive leaders of Sikhism were honored with that title.

Accounts of Guru Nanak's pressing concern for human welfare vary between an acute awareness of human need and a direct vision from God. For sure, he advocated a collage of concerns for spiritual, social, and political conduct. He emphasized equality of persons, fraternal caring, and virtuous behavior. He practiced meditation. He composed literature, especially hymns of praise to divinity.

Guru Nanak kept the Hindu reincarnation and karma teachings. Persons have incarnate souls which are the essential element continuing to live through rebirth. The soul's sought-after destiny is escape from life into reunion with Brahman—escape from this world forever. This thinking was not in accord with Muslim teaching, but Guru Nanak overlooked that, and at the same time held fast to the Muslim belief in one God, Allah.

Guru Nanak relied heavily on the Hindu virtue of bhakti, the way of love for all things and humankind. He applied bhakti as the active, creative, expressive practice of loyalty, truthfulness, temperance, and purity. He taught these virtues as good common sense, rather than arbitrary commandments from God.

He added a lengthy lists of morals. There are four mandatory:

1. Hajamat (no cutting of hair).
2. Halal (no unclean food).
3. Haram (no adultery).
4. Hakka (no tobacco, no intoxicants).

There are more for personal conduct. Some are:

1. Work in service of others.
2. Bathe in holy streams, morning bath for sure.
3. Be baptized.
4. Use sandai incense.
5. Sing hymns.

6. Pray.
7. Meditate.
8. Make pilgrimage to the Golden Temple in Amritsar.

Guru Nanak denied any afterlife. There are no heaven and hell. A person either is here on Earth, or in eternal unity with God. He called unity with God "being in divine court." The court is paradisiacal. Hell is being apart from God. Heaven and hell are conditions of the mind, not actual places. At death, a person returns to God the creator.

Guru Nanak rejected the rituals, offerings, pilgrimages, and plurality of gods practiced by his native religion of Hinduism. He praised the devoted meditation practice of Buddha Siddhartha. Then he brought a new dimension to meditation: it can take the form of service to humankind. Acts of kindness are meritorious. Ethical living is efficacious.

Guru Nanak taught that dying is not to be feared. It is the opportunity to be in God's court. Passage 599 from the holy writ of *Adi Granth* advises followers to realize that if they are in God's court, "the way of death will be easy to tread."

The adherents of Sikhism were in frequent conflict with occupying Muslim authorities, who viewed Sikhism as heresy. According to Islam, Muhammad was the final prophet; this undercut Guru Nanak as having prophetic status. According to Islam, the *Qur'an* was the apex and end of all holy works; Guru Nanak wrote new scripture, the *Adi Granth*.

The fifth Sikh guru, Guru Arjan Dev, in 1606 CE was ordered by the Muslims to cease and desist. He refused to do so, and was tortured to death by Muslim order.

The next leader of Sikhism, Guru Har Gobind, changed the pacific nature of the religion to one of self-defense. He ordered Sikhs to arm themselves and be ready to defend themselves against Muslims or anyone else. Sikhs obeyed. They carried weapons, especially short daggers concealed up their sleeves. The warriors organized into the order of Khalsa. They distinguished themselves with uncut hair on the head and face, a comb in their head hair, short trousers, a steel bracelet, a steel dagger, and followed a total prohibition of wine, tobacco, and drugs. The men used the last name of Singh (lion), and the women used the last name of Kaur (princess).

The ninth Guru also was executed by the Muslims. His successor, Guru Gobind Singh (1666–1708), ruled there would be no more Gurus, thus depriving the Muslims of anyone to murder. He declared that henceforth the Guru would be the holy book itself, the *Adi Granth*. This book is still the literal, total ruler for Sikhs, rather than a human being.

The *Adi Granth* has the advantage of prescribing unchanging conduct for life. It has the disadvantage that not all Sikhs read it exactly the same. The branch of Sikhism called Udasi declares the *Adi Granth* demands Sikhs to live as hermits. The branch called Sahajdhris centers on pacifism. The branch called Nirmalas features monasticism.

The places of worship are called gurdwaras. The main gurdwara is the Golden Temple (Harimandir Sahib) in Amritsar, Punjab. Some of the leaders are called akai takht, granti, guru, jattedar, and yogi.

A unique service to the public is the Langar. After gurdwara worship, which is scheduled by the leader, usually on a Friday, Saturday, or Sunday, a meal is prepared by the group and served free to anyone in the entire area/community no matter what social status, nationality, color, creed, caste, religion, or any other status.

Festivals vary according to country, but all Sikhs celebrate Guru Nanak's birthday (November), Guru Arjan's birthday (December/January), and Vaisakhi (April) as the New Year festival and also as the day the Khalsa was formed.

In 1968 a contingent of Sikhs immigrated to Espanola Valley, New Mexico, United States of America. They were led by Siri Singh Sahib, who was titled as Yogi Bhajan. They practice a bhakti (love) version of the original Guru, Nanak. The number of Sikhs worldwide is approximately thirty million. The ultimate destiny Sikhs pursue is escape from earthly life by returning to God.

SECTION II

Far East: Enjoy

This section presents the Far East religions of Taoism, Confucianism, and Shintoism. They are almost exclusively located in China and Japan. These three religions are different from the four religions of the Middle East. These religions of the Far East call on the people to enjoy life, rather than escape it.

Taoism and Confucianism are Chinese religions that began as government and social reforms. After a few centuries they became so popular as ways of life they were given reverent adoration. Soon they took on the accoutrements of religion. Bear in mind, however, originally they were not religions in the usual sense as, say, the Middle East or Near East religions. The two Chinese religions pay little attention to mythology about gods who judge and reward or punish human behavior. They acknowledge there might be a divine force, called Tao/Dao. The force has its way of conducting the functioning of the universe; sometimes this manner is called the "Mandate of Heaven." The manner of the Mandate is the model for human dynasties.

Shintoism was begun in Japan as a combined nationalistic and religious phenomenon. It was founded as the total way of life for all facets of Japanese living. It was formed in 522 CE, many centuries later than the Chinese religions. It has some of the same aspects as the Chinese religions inasmuch as Japan borrowed extensively from China. The very name, "Shen" plus "Tao," is a combination of the Chinese expression "the way of the gods." Shinto was inspired by Japan's own supreme goddess, Amaterasu. The Japanese religion and government were to rule as if the goddess Amaterasu herself were ruling. Amaterasu was also the grandparent of the Japanese emperors, as well as of the nation itself; therefore, both people and nation are accorded divinity.

Shintoism was jolted about 500 CE by a rapid incursion of Buddhism. It was jolted again in 1945 CE by the loss of Japan in World War II, resulting in a surrender agreement that carried the admission the Japanese emperor and people were not actual relatives of divinity. In spite of these jolts, Shintoism/Shinto carries on today as a viable religion, mainly confined to Japan.

All three Far East religions are intent on providing a good life for people, an enjoyable life, not one desiring to escape from life. Getting older for humans is good. Long life, not a sacrificial life, is good. One life is good, not life after life via reincarnation. An overgeneralized but intriguing term for Far East religions' way of life is "enjoy."

5

Taoism

Taoism began as a remedy for state chaos, then developed into a religion of harmony with the way nature runs the cosmos.

Taoism began in China in the sixth century BCE with the notable person Lao Tzu. Historical information about him is so sketchy that some scholars aver he was a literary creation rather than a real live person. At any rate, he is reported to have lived in the sixth century BCE, being slightly older than Confucius.

According to tradition, Lao Tzu was a very wise minister in the emperor's regime. He was employed as a keeper of court records. He became so stressed over the minutia of his job that he furtively fled town. He mounted his donkey and attempted to ride west over the mountains. He was stopped by the guard at the pass. The guard recognized him as an important figure and refused to let him leave (if the guard let such a well-known high official leave without a direct order from the emperor, the guard could be put to death). Lao Tzu successfully negotiated a departure on the condition that he write down all his wisdom.

It is claimed that he wrote down what has become the sacred scripture of Taoism, the *Tao Te Ching/Dao De Jing*. Evidence is lacking as to whether Lao Tzu actually wrote the *Tao Te Ching* or whether the authors were unrecognized disciples. Whatever the case, the *Tao Te Ching* became the sacred scripture for Taoism. It is said Lao Tzu was never heard from again after the border incident.

Lao Tzu wrote in a cultural continuum. He grew up as a typical Chinese person of his time. Such a person had the background of centuries of culture. The background included multiple divinities who bestowed life and caused the crops to grow. The emperors as well as the people celebrated spring and fall seasons for the sprouting and harvesting of the crops. They welcomed the work of the divinities, sometimes denoted as the "pleasure-controlling Anima."

The multiple divinities were over-lorded by a productive metaphysical force which is dual. The force has a bright power called the Yang and a dark power called the Yin. Yang and Yin do not battle with each other for control of the world (as some other religions have good and evil forces battling), but work in harmony for making life enjoyable. For example, day (bright) and night (dark) do not battle for supremacy; they blend their natures to give growth and rest to humanity and the universe. When they are in harmony, life is happy.

Commensurate with this harmony is longevity. To have the most enjoyment in life, one has to live long. Getting old is good. Getting older is a result of growing wiser. The old are to be venerated for their achievement of growing old. Archaeologists of a century ago usually called this attitude of awe for ancestors "worship." The term worship has given way now to the term "veneration" of the elderly. The elderly can continue to exert influence on their living relatives, so it is beneficial to give them veneration; if neglected, the ancestral spirits might be disgraced and/or become homeless spirits.

In a like vein, the practice of divination is important in order to follow the surest route to longevity. Cracks in a turtle shell, or the lay of a bird's entrails, or the arrangement of stalks of grain, are favorite ways of seeing how to live in order to circumvent misfortune or death. A special book, the *I Ching*, was kept for disseminating these favorite ways.

The writings also promote progeny and prosperity. Progeny are necessary to care for both crops and the elderly. Prosperity provides financial means to care for the crops and the elderly. On a national scale, prolongevity, progeny, and prosperity ensure enjoyable life.

At times in China's history, a regime would come to power and order everyone to believe in some divine power. One such time was in the eleventh century BCE Zhou dynasty. The emperor ordered belief in a god who controlled all human destinies. He called this god Shangdi. This god was the patron ancestor of the Zhou dynasty. Neither Taoism nor Confucianism gave much preference to this declared dynastic divinity.

About the sixth century BCE the wars between the sub-kingdoms of China started what is denoted by historians as the Warring States Period. It was at this time the feudal system of living in China collapsed. The emperor lost central control. The petty-kings fought with each other for preeminence. The chaos was described by a contemporary as so brutal the blood ran as deep as the horses' bridles in Peking.

Into this rift in statehood came Lao Tzu and Confucius. Each presented a way to reestablish the good life in China. Lao Tzu said there was too much government. Confucius said there was too little government.

Lao Tzu, according to the *Tao Te Ching*, recommended a moratorium on legalism, and a return to flowing with the natural forces of the universe. He withdrew from the fast lane of conflicting and constricting decrees and regulations. He countenanced a naturalism described as Wu Wei. Usually this term is translated into English as "quietude." The term also carries with it the meaning of non-action. Governments and people should back off and "go with the flow" more than straining to interfere with the natural process of things. There is a free-flowing spirit in the universe; watch for it and follow. Some scholars think Lao Tzu meant the natural Mandate of Heaven was being distorted by meddling humans. He counseled to regroup; let rulers and people live according to their calmer, happier, natural ways of conduct.

Taoism formulates three vital principles that are to be kept in balance, variously called Three Virtues or Three Jewels or Three Treasures: compassion, moderation, and humility. Also, Taoism emphasizes the doctrine of the meridians, the centers of the natural way the physical bodies of persons work. The meridian theory locates certain energy virtues in the human body. These energy virtues need nurturing in order to live according to nature, that is, according to the natural construction of the human body. Other Taoists add breathing rules. Others ingest powdered dragon bones mixed with moonbeams and mother of pearl in order to nurture well-being. Many practice individual meditation.

In the second century BCE, Lao Tzu's way became so popular with the Han dynasty that the emperor ordered a temple erected to honor Lao Tzu. The date probably was about 195 BCE. Once a temple was built, then a staff was needed to maintain it. In time, rituals and offerings were observed. In time the people at large viewed the Taoist temple as the center of a new religion, Taoism.

Some scholars of the day wondered if the Tao spoken of in the *Tao Te Ching* was a god. After all, there were myths about gods and spirits in Chinese folklore. Taoist doctrine is that Tao is neither a god nor a god-person combined. Tao is the pattern of harmony in the universe. It is present in all things. It is the natural force at work. It works through Yang and Yin. It is the way the entire cosmic order proceeds. When followed it brings harmony which brings the joy of living.

Humans blend with the way of the Tao by living quiet, natural, simple lives. Since Tao is the force of all life, then life itself is the supreme human possession. The *Tao Te Ching* exhorts persons to live naturally as the world force (Tao) proceeds naturally, then "you will know what to do."

Taoist worship is marked with usual accompaniments of religion, such as cleansing, rituals, readings, and offerings, all led by trained persons, with such titles as daoshi, monk, nun, or priest. The leaders are given respect, but the scholars who are wise about the natural providence of life are given higher reverence.

The places of worship are called gong; some places are very elaborate temples with statuary and colorful structures. Gong also includes altars in the home, simple huts, and grottoes.

In the fourth century CE, Buddhists made inroads in China. The pacific nature of Buddhism appealed to the adherents of Taoism. Many Chinese followed precepts of both religions. By the sixth century, Taoism had founded its own monasteries and nunneries in Buddhist style.

After the early days of unity Taoism divided into several groups. One group still popular, the Orthodox Unity, in southern China, follows carefully the standard ways set forth in the *Tao Te Ching*. Another group, the Complete Perfection, in northern China, brings in variant ways and literature. These two groups are active today. From time to time other subgroups flourish.

The ancient culture of China has held festivals still celebrated by nearly every countryman, including Taoists. Taoists participate in the national New Year festival Tet, coming at the end of January or the beginning of February. Tet is marked by house cleaning, entertainment of guests, sumptuous feasts, veneration of gods and ancestors, gift-giving, parades, and firecrackers. Another festival is Pure and Bright, which is a celebration of spring and the renewal of Yang. Still another is the Dragon Boat festival celebrating summer and the renewal of Yin. Another, the autumn festival, celebrates the harvest, and features foods, moon cakes, poetry, and thanksgiving for the abundance of crops. Yet another, the winter festival, celebrates birthdays of heroes, divinities, and saintly religionists. As in many Western countries, All Souls Day in the fall is a time of keeping in good favor with ancestors; it features offerings of foods, flowers, and the lighting of bonfires.

Taoism has no creed. It has no primal divinity. It has no ordained office begun by Lao Tzu and passed down through a mode of succession.

Through the centuries a few popular divinities have been instituted: Shou Hsing, god of long life; Fu Hsing, god of happiness; and Lu Hsing, god or bringer of male children. The pre-Taoist goddess His-Wang-Mu / Heavenly-Empress / Queen-Mother-West, is given folk reverence. She has existed in popular Chinese mythology for thousands of years. She holds the peach which ripens every three thousand years and is eaten by the other gods to continue their immortality.

Taoist-inspired art has become notable. It portrays landscapes. Mountains and streams are in the background, trees—evergreens often—are closer; usually in front is an old master Taoist or a group of people smaller than the nature background, all depicting quietude and the glory of oldness.

Taoism today has an estimated fifty million followers. This is an unconfirmed number. Although the current political regime in China recognizes Taoism as a legitimate entity, it keeps a limit on Taoist activities, including compiling an official count. Whether Taoism is legal or not, whether free or censored, whether originally a social philosophy or a religion, Taoism continues to inspire adherents to enjoy the good life on the good Earth.

6

Confucianism

CONFUCIANISM IS A RELIGION of proper behavior both for persons and state in order to achieve peaceful harmony.

The second Far East religion in our study is Confucianism. It started in the sixth century BCE, not as a religion, but as a social theory to save the Chinese state from disintegration due to the civil unrest.

Confucius was a historical person who lived 551—479 BCE. His real name was K'ung Fu-Tzu. "Confucius" is a mispronunciation that began when foreign forces invaded China. Confucius was born in Qufu, Lu, a small city in a province now renamed Shandong near the mouth of the Yellow River. His father, Kong He, was well-known as a warrior; he was gigantic in size compared to the average Chinese man. He was seventy years old when Confucius was conceived. He died shortly afterward. Confucius was raised by his widowed mother, Yan Zhengzai.

After his father died the family income dropped to the poverty level due to the civil wars and the collapse of the feudal system. Confucius was given free space at school by the village tutor. The curriculum included typical subjects of the time, such as literature, poetry, music, history, hunting, fishing, and archery. Confucius liked school so much that by the age of fifteen he had vowed to become a teacher. He showed great interest in the restoration of academic wisdom as his way to remedy Chinese strife. He became intent on rescuing Chinese life from its social chaos.

Little more is heard about him until age twenty-seven, when he was employed in the Lu court. Less is heard about him until age fifty when he won a post as police commissioner. He left that job in a year. He spent the rest of his occupational years seeking a political post through which he could bring glory back to his people. He did not find such a position.

He continued developing his teaching on good government. Instead of formulating a prestigious plan, he believed Chinese civilization would be best served by refining conduct. He posited propriety as the key. Confucius surmised that if people act properly toward each other, life would be enjoyable for individuals, families, and the state. He chose the Chinese word *li* to indicate propriety. Often propriety is further denoted as *jen/ren*. "Human heartedness" is a smooth translation of this term. People should practice respect toward one another. People should be courteous toward one another. He taught that people should love one another. His rule of thumb was "what you do not want done to you, do not do unto others." He listed Five Relationships of Propriety:

1. Father to son: father, kindness; son, family loyalty.
2. Older brother to younger brother: older, geniality; younger, humility.
3. Husband to wife: husband, virtue; wife, obedience.
4. Older to younger: older, consideration; younger, deference.
5. Ruler to subject: ruler, benevolence; subject, loyalty.

Confucius believed people have the native ability to practice propriety. People are created in the positive mode. People are created with natural goodness. Practice of these Five Relationships would fulfill the meshing of the ancient Chinese natural forces of Yang and Yin for happy harmony.

Confucius had an ambivalent attitude toward divine assistance that would aid persons to conduct themselves with propriety. He seemed to accept the realm of divinities in the ancient Chinese manner: there may well be divinities, but they are not immanent or personal; nor are they judgmental or threatening. The divinities of heaven have their own business to conduct.

One of Confucius' later disciples, Mengzi/Mencius (ca. 372—289), was a charismatic schoolman who taught the way of Confucius with great effectiveness. He was noted for affirming Confucius' contention that human nature is good and able. Humans have the power to rectify personal unhappiness. Humans could govern the state with such wisdom that China would be a notable realm of enjoyment.

As in Taoism, under the Han dynasty, probably around 200 BCE, a temple was built to honor Confucius. Rituals, writings, sacrifices, offerings, and conduct were fashioned. Leaders perpetuated reverence for the Confucian way. Confucianism became a nationally recognized religion.

The general features of Confucianism are distinct from some key concepts of the other religions treated in this book. Confucianism has no personal divinity who converses with humans. It has no divine director of human history. It has no saviors. It has no coming messiah. It has no succession line of ordained clergy. It has no creed.

However, Confucianism does have some features that the other religions have. It has public sites of worship called temples, and sacred rooms in homes in which altars have been erected. It has leaders called pastors, priests, or professors. It has literature which has become the sacred scripture: the *Four Chinese Classics*, the *Analects*, and *Mencius*. It has rituals of reverence for ancestors (Confucius observed a three year wake for his mother when she died). It makes use of prayer for good outcomes. It encourages works of art and the building of exquisite temples. It has a significant number of adherents, about six million.

In our time Confucianism is not respected as a religion by the current Peoples' Republic of China government, but Confucians carry on in whatever ways possible. Notably, Confucians join all China in celebrating the festivals observed from ancient times, principally Tet (New Year), Qingminga (Spring), Duanwu/Tuen Ng (Summer), Tet Trung Thu (Autumn), and Qing Ming Jie (All Souls' Day). Confucius' birthday is celebrated on September 28.

Confucianism offers the notable religion values of social community, proper conduct, compassionate care, and way-of-life culture. It is a bright and happy religion for life on Earth. It is a religion for living now. It has little to say about afterlife. It is a humanly possible action of following rules of propriety to bring harmony to persons and the state. It is for people to enjoy life on Earth.

7

Shintoism

SHINTOISM/SHINTO IS A RELIGION of nationalism, created by and for Japan.

Shinto was formulated comparatively late in the Common Era, many centuries after Taoism and Confucianism, and several millennia after the ancient religions of China. The beginning date for the religion of Shintoism is observed as 522 CE, only about fifteen hundred years ago.

Why Shintoism is so late coming has been given several answers by researchers. One answer is the gods revealed Shintoism on their own schedule and decreed its formation; end of search, closed. Two is Buddhism was making such inroads in Japan in the sixth century CE that native religion leaders composed Shintoism in order to preserve cultural ways. Three is small Japan had an inferiority complex, being so close to behemoth China, so its leaders devised a religion to give Japan nationalistic self-identity. The name "Shinto" is a Japanese adaptation of two Chinese terms, *Shen* and *Tao*. In Japanese these are phrased as Kami-no-michi. Shinto is a religion that is appropriate for Japan, but does not have a universal mission to convert the world.

The sacred scriptures of Shintoism, *Kojiki* and *Nihongi*, were composed in the seventh and eighth centuries CE. They purport to describe mythical origins for Shintoism that go all the way back to the beginning of time. At the origin of creation there were many gods already in the heavenly realm. They ran the universe. They were given the general name of Kami.

One account describes the evolution of Shintoism in this way. The divine family included the parents, Izanagi and Izanami. They gave birth to a son from Izanagi's right eye, Tsukuyomi. They gave birth to another son when Izanagi washed his nose, Susano-O. They gave birth to a daughter from his left eye, Amaterasu. Amaterasu and Tsukuyomi picnicked with the goddess of food, Uke Mochi. She served the food so disgustingly Tsukuyomi killed her. Amaterasu was appalled and banished Tsukuyomi to a part of the heavens where he created day and night. Susano-O was a rascally sort of fellow in charge of the seas. Susano-O once in his rascally mood, killed and skinned Amaterasu's pony. Amaterasu skirmished with him. He lured her into a cave and shut the exit.

With Amaterasu imprisoned, the world was in danger of extinction, for Amaterasu furnished the sun. The other hundreds of Kamis begged her to use her divine power to break loose and come out, but to no avail. Then the Kamis gathered roosters (whose crowing precedes the dawn) and the Yata no Kagami (an eight-handed mirror) and glittering jewels, and positioned them on a sakaki tree in front of the cave. The goddess Ama-no-Uzume began to dance on an upturned tub, partially disrobing herself, which so delighted the assembled gods that they roared with laughter. They laughed so loudly that Amaterasu became curious. Amaterasu opened the door to her internment slowly to peek outside. The cocks saw her light and began to crow. The Yasakani no Magatama Jewels glittered, and the Mirror hanging on the tree reflected her light. She saw her own reflection and thought there must be someone or something equal to herself illuminating the world. As she opened the door a little wider, the deity Ama-no-Tajikara-wo-no-Kami, who was waiting behind the door, pulled Amaterasu out of the cave and quickly threw a shimenawa (sacred rope of rice straw) before the entrance to prevent her from returning to hiding. Amaterasu agreed to remain in the visible world and never again withdraw.

Amaterasu's son, Ame-no-Oshi-ho-Mimi, had a son named Ninigi no Mikoto. Amaterasu sent Ninigi to Earth, entrusting him with the sacred regalia of Japanese lore, consisting of the Yata no Kagami (the eight-handed mirror) and the Yasakani no Magatama (the curved jewels); also the Kusanagi no Tsurugi (the sword from Susano-O that had been given to her by Susano-O after he conquered the Orochi Dragon). Ninigi descended to Earth and at once set about taming the unruly world. Not long afterward, Ninigi married Kono-Hana-Sakuya-Hime (Princess-Blossoming-Brilliantly-as-the-Flowers-of-Trees), the daughter of the mountain god Oyamatsumi-no-Kami. They had a son O-no-susori-no-Mikoto, the ancestor of Jimmu Tenno, the first emperor of Japan. Consequently, the people of Japan are direct descendants of the divinely-birthed emperor Jimmu Tenno. Thus, all Japanese are children of divinity.

Amaterasu was enthroned as the central divinity of Shintoism. She is well known the world over as the emblazoned symbol on the Japanese flag. Besides being the ancestral goddess and the goddess of sun itself, Amaterasu is credited also with inventing the cultivation of rice and wheat, the use of silkworms, and weaving with a loom.

Another account of prehistoric metaphysical origination again features Izanagi and Izanami. Before humans, there was only a germ of life in the universe. This germ began to mix things around and around until the heavier part sank and the lighter part rose. A muddy sea covered the entire Earth. One day the gods Izanagi and Izanami were walking along and looked down on the sea and wondered what was beneath it. Izanagi thrust his staff into the muddy sea. As he pulled it up some clumps of mud fell back into the sea. They began to harden and grow until they became the islands of Japan. The two gods descended to these islands and began to explore, each going in different directions. They created all kinds of plants.

In this version of origins Izanagi and Izanami decided to marry and have children to inhabit the land. The first child Izanami bore was a girl of radiant beauty. The gods decided she was too beautiful to live in Japan, so they put her up in the sky and she became the sun, Amaterasu. Their second daughter, Tsuki-yami, became the moon. Their third child, unruly Susano-O, was sentenced to the sea, where he created storms.

Then Izanagi and Izanami artfully fashioned the trees, mountains, valleys, streams, winds, and other natural features of Japan with gods and goddesses. Thus, not only the emperors but also the islands and all the natural features, especially the mountains and streams, and the plants and animals were divinely created.

The religion of Shintoism took official form in the sixth century CE. A temple was erected especially to honor Amaterasu at Ise, Mie. There Amaterasu is represented by the Mirror, the Jewel, and the Sword, the three Japanese imperial regalia. It is customary for Shinto believers to make a pilgrimage to the shrine at least once in a lifetime. A joyous festival for Amaterasu is celebrated every July 17. Her coming out of the cave is celebrated on December 21.

Shintoism reverences ancestors, nation, and geographical features. Besides alters at mountains and streams, family homes may have a holy room where prayers are offered, scriptures are read, and symbols are displayed. Businesses may set aside a room for rituals of worship. Public places of worship are called shrines or temples, with a Japanese designation of jinga. Usually jinga are entered through a gateway called a torii, a structure with posts and a crossbar with turned-up ends.

Jinga are visited mostly on holidays or when some blessing is desired. A typical jinga shrine has an outer area for anyone of any religion who would meditate, pray, or give offerings in honor of the Kami. The jinga also has an inner shrine for priests and government officials. There are jinga shrines for pregnant women who want a safe delivery, ones for fishermen to return safely from the sea, and ones for achieving sexual gratification. Small shrines are common in homes and offices; prayers in these implore the gods to ward off unhappiness, dispel evil spirits, obviate hunger, and cure disease. Funerals do not take place in Shinto shrines, as death is considered impure.

Upon entering a jinga, or a private home, persons are expected to show reverence by removing their shoes. In Shinto homes a god-shelf, called a Kami-dana, may hold photos or items of ancestors or other Kami. The oldest person makes sure food is regularly offered to the Kami inasmuch as gods, too, must be nourished.

A general term for Shinto leaders is priest. Some specific denotations are daiguji, guji, gonguji. saishu, shaman, and shinshoku.

They direct rituals of purification, prayers, readings of sacred scripture, and the receiving of offerings. A shaman who has direct communication with Kami may conduct séances with the gods as a worship feature or privately at the request of a member. Shrine officials conduct weddings and milestone events for children.

The shrine at Ise is the defining structure of Shinto. It is regarded with holy awe. It receives great numbers of pilgrims. Shinto members are urged to visit this shrine at least once during their lifetime. Ise is especially popular as a rallying place for renewal of patriotic allegiance to Japan. A close second shrine for high admiration is Mount Fuji.

Various popular gods have been given reverence through the ages. Others besides the gods may be enshrined, such as heroes, ancestors, and officials, as well as natural sites and virtues—all can be Kami. Some of the special Kami are:

- Benzaiten—love goddess.
- Bishamonten—war.
- Hotei-Oshu—generosity.
- Jurojin—long life.
- Fukurokuju—long life number two.
- Daikoku—wealth.
- Ebisu—work.
- Tenjin—divinized ninth-century scholar, learning.

The holy writings give an even more colorful list of hundreds of Kami. They have lengthy names which integrate geographical features of Japan, or virtues, or other respected entities. Names of a very few of them are:

> Deity Great-Ocean-Possessor, Deity Mud-Earth-Lady,
> Deity Oh-Awful-Lady, Deity Rock-Nest-Princess,
> Heavenly-Eternally-Standing-Deity,
> Luxuriant Integrating-Master-Deity,
> Master-of-the-Centre-of-Heaven,
> Pleasant-Reed-Shoot-Deity, and Prince-Elder-Deity.

Festivals are joyously celebrated by all of Japan whether in or out of official Shinto count. Some major celebrations are:

- Shogatsu: January 1–6, New Year, foods, offerings to honor ancestors.
- Niiname-sai: November 23 and 24, harvest.
- Hatsumiyamairi: a child's first worship at a shrine.
- Sichi-go-san: November 15, 7–5–3, for boys age 5, girls ages 3 and 7.
- Gion Matsuri: July 13–17, honoring the plague-ending emperor of 869 CE.

A growing group of Shintoists are being attracted in our time by a branch called Tenrikyo/Tenriism. It originated with the teachings of a nineteenth-century woman, Nakayama Miki/Oyasama. Tenrikyo's aim is to teach and promote the Joyous Life, which is cultivated through acts of charity and mindfulness. Tenrikyo supports sixteen thousand eight hundred thirty-three locally managed "churches" in Japan, the construction and maintenance of the Oyasato-Yakata (Headquarters) in Tenri, Nara, and various community-focused organizations. It claims about two million followers.

Shintoism allows variations as long as Amaterasu and the nation are honored. There are current vogues such as mountain reverence, faith healing, personal improvement, asceticism, and meditation.

Orthodox Shintoism made a few notable blends with Buddhism over the years. One is Zen, a deep meditative form. Another is Pure Land, which looks toward afterlife in an ideal state. Still other schools are Nichiren and Soka Gokkai.

"Saving face" is a traditional concept among Japanese. Persons are supposed to act in harmony with each other. If they do not so act, they interrupt the processes of nature and incur the transgression of not saving face. A person restores face by doing all possible actions to regain harmony with the offended one, even to the point of giving of life. Losing face is called "shame," rather than "sin" as in a divinity-directed religion. Losing face is not an offense against a deity, but against another person.

The number of adherents of Shintoism is problematic. The number of four million is usually given, but Shinto is so deeply embedded in Japanese culture that quite probably all of the one hundred twenty-seven million people of the islands have some relationship to, or awareness of, Shintoism. It is common for Japanese people to lean toward Buddhism when it comes to such matters as belief in afterlife, funerary functions, and meditation, yet participate in Shinto fashion in the age-long traditions and festivals of the nation.

Shintoism sees life through a positive scope. Shinto teaches that all Japanese can and ought to revere the Kami and the nation, observe the traditional festivals, raise happy families, and enjoy their days on Earth.

SECTION III

Near East: Endure

This section treats the four religions of the Near East: Judaism, Christianity, Islam, and Baha'i.

These four proclaim that there is one almighty God who informs their origin, meaning, and destiny. God is called by various names, El, Yahweh, Adonai, Lord, or Allah, but is the same, the one and only, God.

These four religions claim to be divinely revealed and guided. They claim their person-like God talked with their primary persons and gave birth to their religions: for Judaism, Moses, about 1250 BCE; for Christianity, Jesus, first century CE; for Islam, Muhammad, 610 CE; and for Baha'i, Husayn, 1863 CE. In all they span over three thousand years.

It might be assumed since God recruited these primary persons, then God would bless them with immunity from life's ills.

However, all four had to endure mighty misfortunes. Moses for Judaism was pursued by the Egyptian pharaoh's troops who would have destroyed him; he then had to wander in the desert for forty years; he then was barred from entering his own promised land. Jesus for Christianity—while not the founder of Christianity, is its central figure—was betrayed and crucified. Muhammad for Islam had to fight military battles, was wounded in one, barely survived, had to recover from a dinner poisoning, and was faced with successor unrest that left out his own son-in-law. Husayn for Baha'i was imprisoned, was exiled from home and country time after time, and his introductory predecessor was murdered by a firing squad. Nevertheless their bequests to world history demonstrate the remarkable characteristic of Near East religions for their adherents: endure.

Besides the primary figures, each of these four religions have many illustrious persons who received from divinity, and/or composed themselves, libraries of religion writings, some of the compositions so distinguished that they have been designated "sacred scriptures."

These four religions practice rituals that are typical of religions. They furnish communities of faith that sustain their adherents. Their members care for one another as family. They set forth codes of conduct for disciples to follow. They institute life-enhancing cultural customs that give their followers self-identity.

All four of these religions began in or around the Near East countries of modern Israel, Iran, Iraq, and Saudi Arabia. Today their members reside in countries worldwide. Their members constitute the huge majority of adherents in all of organized religion; when added together their number totals over one-half of Earth's current seven billion population.

8

Judaism

JUDAISM IS BASED ON a divinely revealed commission to share with God the establishment of the reign of God on Earth.

Judaism is a highly influential religion related in history to a family, a tribe, a nation, and a state. The family is that of Abraham. The tribe is that of Hebrew. The nation is that of Jew. The state is that of Israel. The historical period for this stream is about four thousand years.

Abram/Abraham is recorded in sacred scripture as talking with God about his family's destiny around the year 1850 BCE. Abraham lived in Iraq and was directed by God/El to go to nearby Canaan (now most of Israel) and settle. Canaan was a sparsely settled country in the Near East Mediterranean area. Abraham was assured by El that this territory would be his "promised land." The conversation between El and Abraham did not result in a formal agreement, rather in a kind of handshake relationship. On Abraham's side, he would obey El. On El's side he would "bless" Abraham with homeland, nationhood, fame, and being a benefit to all the world. El and Abraham would keep company with each other.

Abraham's family was probably about fifty persons counting family and attendants. His tribe, named Hebrews, prospered and grew. After Abraham died, the Hebrews were led by his grandson Jacob.

Jacob's blessed time in the promised land was interrupted by a baneful time of drought. One year the crops were so poor that some of his kin migrated to Egypt, where the Nile Valley produced an abundance of grain. In Egypt, to distinguish the Hebrew line from native Egyptians, another name, "Israel," was used by Abraham's kin. The Israelites prospered in Egypt. They became so numerous that after scores of years running into the hundreds, the Pharaoh enslaved them lest they get imperialistic notions. The Israelites are presumed to have kept at least some elements of their religion while in Egypt, such as offering, prayer, adoration of their divinity, and a sense of being a designated people.

Note that hundreds of years pass. About the year 1250 BCE a messianic figure was chosen by God (now called Yahweh/YHWH) to carry on the religion tradition. Yahweh called Moses to the task of freeing the enslaved Israelites and taking them back to their promised land where they could practice the ways of God without Egyptian interference. Moses led the Israelites out of Egypt, and across the Sinai Peninsula toward Canaan/Israel. How many Israelites there were at this time is uncertain, but at least enough to threaten petty kings along the way. There were so many that Moses had difficulty keeping them civil out in the wilds of the Sinai desert. The practice of companying with God and the ways of God's reign were compromised by the people on a notable occasion when they worshipped an idol.

Moses believed that Yahweh stepped in and called him to Mount Sinai to reveal to him ten basic rules for the people's conduct:

1. You shall not have other gods before me.
2. You shall not worship an idol.
3. You shall not swear by my name and then lie.
4. You shall remember to rest on the Sabbath.
5. You shall honor your father and mother.
6. You shall not murder.
7. You shall not commit adultery.
8. You shall not steal.
9. You shall not give false witness.
10. You shall not covet a neighbor's possessions.

These Ten Commandments were adopted as the norms for the people, both politically and religiously. In centuries to follow six hundred three more commandments were given by Yahweh, or composed by the Israelite community, covering the many aspects of daily living from food to marriage to parenting to animal care, and myriad other topics, as well as the worship of Yahweh. The commandments were gathered and denominated the *Torah / Law of Moses*. They were made the first section of Judaism's sacred scripture, the *Tanakh*.

Moses died on the way back home. His generals led the Israelites back into the promised land. The order of conduct they set up in Israel was tribal, named after patriarch Jacob's twelve sons. One of the sons was Judah. The territory of Judah was called "Judea." Through a long series of historic events a descendent of Judah was identified as "Yehudah." In time, this became the common name "Jew" translated into English.

The descendants of Judah led in continuing the religion. They worshipped Yahweh at significant landmarks or special enclosures with praises, prayers, and offerings. They commissioned priests to guide their worship. Life among them was a whole cloth: unity of religion and state.

As the years passed, a sense of the majesty of God grew so sacred in the people's minds that they set aside the general nomenclature of "God," and addressed him generically as "Adonai" or "Lord." The Israelites continued to worship at altars built of rocks, or at important wells, or in tented tabernacles, or on mountains such as Sinai, where Moses received the Ten Commandments.

The people at times committed apostasy by not companying with the divinity of their ancestors, but worshipping the gods of other cultures, or worshipping images of animals. Apostasy usually occurred when crops failed or other misfortunes plagued the people, and they doubted divine power to help them endure.

Conditions in Israel were at a low ebb when another messianic figure was divinely called to preserve the ways of the Lord. David, about the year 1000 BCE, was selected by God to refresh the close relationship the early patriarchs had with God. David responded by renewing allegiance to the reign of the Lord by organizing a mighty state, rebuilding Jerusalem into the capitol city, and planning a stupendous worship center. David himself was praised by God as "a man after my own heart." It may have been about this time that reverence of the Lord became so increased that the scholars began writing the divine name as "G-d."

David's son, Solomon, built the planned worship center in Jerusalem, the Temple, atop the rocky site of Abraham's redoubtable sacrifice of Isaac. It was a magnificent structure. Worshippers were awed at it. Tourists came to gaze at it. The Temple was decreed to be the singular center of the worship of G-d. Orders of priests cleansed themselves with water and then dramatically sacrificed animals on its pyre as worship to G-d. The people gave offerings of money and produce to show their allegiance to G-d. The worshippers chanted and sang psalms of praise. They listened to a class of speakers called "prophets" who praised persons who kept the commandments in the *Torah* and denounced the breakers of the commandments. The august role of the Temple was that G-d himself was housed therein.

The civilization stemming from the Hebrews continued until about 700 BCE, when a neighboring superpower, Assyria, conquered Israel and destroyed the Temple. The religion almost faltered without its independent promised land and its magnificent Temple, but its leaders adroitly kept it going by gathering worshippers in groups called synagogues. Many citizens left Israel, either by choice or by force of Assyria, and these dispersed ones composed a category of Diaspora Jews. The remaining Israelites regrouped and rebuilt their religion center, the second Temple, completed about the year 515 BCE.

For the next six hundred years the people had their ups and downs as a religiopolitical state, often suffering evils at the hands of other countries. Sometimes they themselves brought misfortunes by their apostasy from G-d. The religion was continued as it had been, except some fissures were formed by parties with special interests.

By 70 CE, Israel had been annexed by the superpower Rome. One Israelite party resented the Roman rule to the point of initiating military action. These party-led Israelites were no match for Rome. The state and the second Temple in which the religion was centered were obliterated by the Roman army. The Romans enslaved or killed every Jew they could catch. The Jews who escaped are called those of the second Diaspora.

One small party survived and resettled in Jamnia, on the coast of Israel. The rest of the dispersed Jews resettled in Europe, Asia, and Africa. The group in Jamnia was led by Yochanan ben Zakkai. Yochanan's dates were 30–90 CE, although some say he lived much longer into the second century. Yochanan assembled a group of scholars and together they preserved the sacred scriptures now fully gathered, the *Tanakh*. Arguably, they preserved the religion itself.

Judaism today is led by scholars who track Yochanan, rather than being led by patriarchs, prophets, or kings. The scholars are called rabbis/rebbes. The rabbis at Jamnia concluded that Judaism was best as given by G-d to Moses in the *Torah / Law of Moses*. The work of interpreting the *Torah* for contemporary times continues to this day.

The rabbis are the authorities for Judaism on the human side. G-d is still the authority on the divine side; this detente is a kind of reenactment of the original Abraham and El relationship. The rabbis continue conversations with G-d about how to endure in a world often unfriendly but yearning for the full reign of G-d on Earth. The rabbis perform the official duties of Judaism. The rabbis (usually male, but an increasing number of females) are highly trained interpreters of conduct according to the *Law of Moses*. Rabbis also study concertedly the rest of the sacred scriptures, the *Tanakh*. Rabbis also are the priestly functionaries who lead the rituals. Rabbis also are the clergy of Judaism as recognized by secular governments. Rabbis also are the ones who care for the congregations of the people of Judaism.

Judaism has evolved into one of the most highly influential world religions. It worships one and only one, personal divinity, G-d, who empowers the adherents to endure evils, even of the worst kind. The religion places high duty on demonstrating the ways given by G-d to all the world. Judaism has the high hope of establishing what some call the "kingdom" of G-d, or the reign of G-d, fully in all the Earth. Judaism no longer has a centering temple, since Islam has usurped the very site of the original temple. Rather, Judaism is enlivened in congregations of synagogues throughout the world.

Judaism continues some of the rituals from of old, notably circumcision of male babies as a sign of their Jewishness and Judaism-ness. The animal sacrifices have given way to monetary gifts or service offerings. The confirmation services of bar mitzvah for boys has been matched with bat mitzvah for girls, celebrating boys and girls becoming men and women of the congregation.

Judaism today has groups within it who interpret the literature and religion slightly differently from each other. The most prolific of these groups are three: Orthodox, Conservative, and Reform. There are smaller groups such as Reconstructionist and Fundamentalist. There are secular Jews who are blood-related, but who do not practice Judaism.

The number of practicing Jews in the world today is about seventeen million. The number of persons who observe Judaism by weekly attendance at a synagogue is somewhat less. The number who keep some of the rituals on food, circumcision, Sabbath rest, and ancestor reverence, is nearer the seventeen million. Judaism keeps its own, rather than striving for converts.

From 70 CE to 1948 CE the Jews had no promised land. They maintained their culture wherever they went, with the conundrum of how to integrate it with the ways of the countries to which they had dispersed. Judaism and Jews have been welcomed or persecuted in those countries where they settled in varying degrees. In 1948 CE, the Jewish state was reestablished in the promised land. There the religion is practiced freely. It is, however, among the foremost in tolerance of and cooperation with other religions.

Judaism has a number of exclusive features. One is the calendar. It begins with the creation of the world dated 3760 BCE. The months are based on the phases of the moon. The number of days in a year is three hundred fifty-seven. An intercalary month is added periodically in order to match the solar calendar. The religion calendar begins with the month Tishri in solar September/October. The civil calendar begins with the month Nisan in solar March/April.

Another feature of Judaism is the holy days and festivals. Shabbat is the weekly holy day, from sundown Friday to sundown Saturday. It is marked with Kiddush prayer of sanctification, special wine and bread, lighting of candles, reading from the *Tanakh*, best food of the week, guests, attendance at a synagogue, and family togetherness. Major festivals are Rosh Hashanah (New Year), Yom Kippur (Day of Atonement), Sukkot (Feast of Booths/Tabernacles), Chanukah (Rededication of the Temple), Purim (Commemoration of Esther), Pesach (Passover), Shavuot (Pentecost), Tisha B'Av (Destruction of First Temple), and Yom HaShoah (Holocaust).

Another feature involves food. Food allowed is called kosher. There are detailed directions on what is allowed and what is not allowed. General guidelines for what is allowed are most plants, meats if bled properly, certain birds and fish, and meat and milk separately. Allowed examples are apple, cattle, chicken, flounder, goat, grasshopper, herring, sheep, and spinach. Some not allowed examples are ant, dog, eel, horse, lasagna, pig, shellfish, snake, and vulture.

One of El's promises to Abraham was that Abraham's descendants would be a blessing to all the world. In fulfillment of that promise, Jews (some practicing Judaism, some not) have bequeathed to the world the Abraham-mentioned blessing as authors, scientists, financiers, scholars, theologians, musicians, comedians, dramatists—just a short list. Furthermore, Judaism is the parent to three of the other great religions of the world: Christianity, Islam, and Baha'i. Furthermore, Judaism enlivens the high task of establishing the reign of G-d on Earth.

Judaism is the continuing expression of the divinely revealed origin, meaning, and destiny of life to its forebears. Jews and Judaism endure. They can sing with the ancient psalmist from chapter 23 of the *Tanakh* that even though the faithful must travel paths through dark valleys, they need not fear any evil, for the Lord will care for them on their pilgrimage.

Jews and Judaism have been dealt evils of slavery, burning of their temple, destruction of their homeland, diasporas, the Holocaust, and anti-Semitism. Nevertheless, Jews and Judaism endure. Judaism continues the work of establishing the ideal civilization/reign of G-d on Earth. It confidently proclaims that those who endure in this mission shall see it finally done.

9

Christianity

CHRISTIANITY PROCLAIMS THAT ITS members shall be divinely blessed in order to endure the vicissitudes of earthly life, and then will be rewarded with eternal afterlife in heaven.

Christianity is the child of Judaism. Christianity inherited many of the beliefs and practices of Judaism, but most significantly it added Jesus as a divine messiah.

Christianity is different from all other religions, except Hinduism, in the respect that it had no founding person. In Christianity the central figure is Jesus, but he was cut short while still a member of his native religion of Judaism. He was executed before his way of doing things was organized as a new religion. Nevertheless, Jesus is the indispensable person at the center of Christianity.

Jesus bar Joseph was born about 6 BCE and died about 29 CE. He was born into a family of Jews that had connections back to King David. David was a messianic figure in Judaism who reunited the people of the promised land in matters both of state and religion at a time of nadir. Any messianic figure who might appear later would benefit by being related to the house of David. Jesus was.

He was born a thousand years later than David, when Israel was again in needy times. The state of Israel had been absorbed into the Roman Empire. It was no longer an independent state.

Israelites/Jews longed to be a free state again. Some Jews bided their time with the Roman rule. Others wanted fast action to rid the country of the Romans. A significant party of Zealots believed they could oust the Romans by themselves, or preferably, with unlimited divine militia and chariots.

Jesus largely ignored the Roman problem. Jesus concentrated on the religion problem. The religion of Israel had not succeeded in a hoped-for way: it had not brought the reign of God fully into the world. Jesus castigated the Judaism leaders of his day for basking in privileged complacency. Jesus saw the people at large as having no shepherd to lead them. Jesus treated his native Judaism as if it had grown stale and needed renewing.

Jesus journeyed to a place on the Jordan River in Israel where John bar Zecharias was entreating the Israelites/Jews to repent of their ignoring the commission of God. John announced that the fulfillment of the kingdom of God was on the cusp. It was ready for fulfillment if only the people would exert concerted effort in godly living. Jesus was baptized into John's movement.

He echoed John's preaching that the kingdom/reign of God on Earth was on the verge of actuality if people would return to companying with God. Jesus gave his own interpretations of what kinds of people would be admitted to the kingdom of God. The descriptions are reported in the early chapters of the *New Testament* as "Beatitudes": people who show need of God, need of consolation, gentleness of spirit, righteousness, mercy, purity of heart, peacefulness; or people who have suffered because they stood for what is right. Jesus often urged listeners to practice love toward one another.

Jesus worked as an itinerant preacher throughout his home state of Galilee. He became a popular figure with the crowds. One story is told that at least five thousand people rallied for him on a hillside. Other stories add that Jesus spectacularly healed people of diseases and bested the forces of nature. He reached beyond Galilee to persons in adjoining Samaria and Syria as if God's reign could include them. He welcomed women and children to his audiences.

Jesus pulled at the seams of his native religion, Judaism. He worked a few times on the Sabbath doing good deeds for people, an abrogation of the fourth of Judaism's Ten Commandments. He

publicly uttered caustic words against the establishment leaders of
Judaism for having more loyalty to their comfortable positions of
power, rather than demonstrating the ways of the reign of God. He
wept over the lethargy of the capitol Jerusalem that it would not
realize the spiritual apostasy in which it lounged.

When Jesus was in his thirties, he journeyed to the center of
Judaism, Jerusalem, apparently to plead the case for getting serious
about practicing God's order for society at its best. After a series
of episodes that are not entirely clear, he offended both the Jewish
establishment and the Roman overlordship and was put to death by
crucifixion.

After the Crucifixion, the close disciples of Jesus took up his
cause. They exhorted their fellow Jews to emulate the religion-
broadening Way of Jesus. Then, in a bold move, they proclaimed
Jesus was a messianic figure after the manner of David, Moses, and
Abraham. They asserted Jesus should be addressed as Messiah. In
the commercial language of the day, Greek, Messiah translates as
"Christ." The disciples had spotty success.

Then a person came onto the scene who was not one of the
close original twelve disciples of Jesus, but one who claimed to have
had a traumatic talk with Jesus. This one was Saul/Paul from Tar-
sus, Cilicia (now Turkey). Paul claimed Jesus informed him that
he (Jesus) had been raised from the dead and had ascended to the
heavens to be with God. Paul was convinced by Jesus to proclaim
the Jesus Way as the necessary revision of established Judaism in
order to realize the full reign of God on Earth.

Paul proclaimed that Jesus was more than a human Messiah;
he also was a divine Messiah. Jesus was not only the perfect person
on Earth, but also the perfect person of God. Furthermore, Paul
claimed Jesus chose to sacrifice himself as the required perfect offering to ameliorate a perfect God.

Paul was a trained scholar and adherent of Judaism. He ap-
proached enclaves of Judaism first to tell them his convictions
about Jesus. He found it difficult to get many adherents from nor-
mative Judaism to accept his version of the Way of Jesus. Paul then
did the unthinkable as far as his native religion went. He invited
non-Jews, Gentiles, to join the Jesus Way directly, without first

becoming converts to Judaism. Paul moved the Jesus Way from what might have been just a party within Judaism to what would become shortly a world religion. His move took advantage of the fact the Gentile audience was about fifty times larger than the entire Jewish population.

Paul and his assistants traveled throughout the southeastern Mediterranean countries preaching the gospel of Jesus. They won followers in major cities of the region. They organized the believers in congregations similar in structure to the synagogues known in Judaism. These groups soon were called churches. Their members were distinguished by the nickname "Christ-ians." They met for worship daily, then on Sundays as the new "sabbbath."

Christians were illegalized by the ruling Roman government. Christians were charged with abandoning the traditional Roman gods, which made them atheists in religion and suspect seditionists to the Empire. They were persecuted and prosecuted by the Roman authorities. For the next nearly three hundred years Christians were outlawed under Roman rule. Where Roman law was applied tightly, Christians had to tread a narrow path to avoid arrest and punishment. Several Christian leaders were publicly condemned and martyred. Many Christians in the city of Rome, and by the end of the first century there were quite a few, sought safety in the dank catacombs underground in Rome.

In the fourth century CE, the status of Christianity was reversed by the Roman Emperor Constantine. He changed his religion from the old Roman gods to Christianity. Thousands of Romans eagerly mimicked Constantine's example. Thousands in Europe, western Asia, and northeastern Africa followed suit.

By the fifth century CE, Christianity had spread widely. The Christians in Europe called themselves the Catholic Church, with their center in Rome. The Christians in Asia called themselves the Orthodox Church, with their center in Constantinople. The Christians in Africa called themselves the Coptic Church, with their center in Egypt.

Christianity remained a shakily unified religion until 451 CE, when the Coptic Church formally severed ties with the Catholic Church over theological and authority issues. Today the Coptic

Church is headquartered in Alexandria, Egypt, and goes also by the formal title Christian Coptic Orthodox Church. This Church elects its own pope.

In 1054, the churches in Asia parted fellowship with the Roman See. Today they are centered in Constantinople, Turkey, and go by optional titles of Eastern Orthodox Church, or Greek Orthodox Church, or Holy Orthodox Catholic and Apostolic Church. This Church elects its own leader, called the patriarch.

The Church in Europe has kept its center in Rome with its head, the pope. It is called also the Western Church, or Roman Church, or Latin Church, or Catholic Church, or Roman Catholic Church, or One Holy Catholic and Apostolic Church.

In 1517 the church headquartered in Rome and churches in Germany disputed with each other over doctrine, authority, and ritual matters. The two groups broke official relationship. The German churches began the Protestant Reformation. One of the Reformation tenets was freedom of individuals to read and interpret the Christian sacred scripture (*New Testament*) in their own ways; they took this seriously. Today there are over two hundred types of Protestants, but all retain their allegiance to Christ Jesus. Protestant churches have spread throughout the world.

In the sixteenth century, King Henry VIII of England and the Roman Catholic Pope Clement VII sparred over marriage rites. When the Pope refused to grant the King a divorce, the King decreed that the churches in England would break their allegiance to Rome and go their own way. The King declared himself the head of the churches in England, and in 1534, led the English congregations in the organizing of their own hierarchy known as the Church of England / Anglican Church.

All five branches of Christianity have organized para-groups, such as monks, nuns, and fraternal orders. All the branches sponsor schools, hospitals, clinics, and other charitable services. The Roman Catholic Church maintains a secular city in Italy, the Vatican.

The theology of Christianity has evolved at the hands of councils and leaders. Two points are unique to Christianity. The first is the nature of Jesus: was Jesus human or divine? Currently the dogma for the nature of Jesus is he was both fully human and fully divine. The fully human consisted of his short life in Israel. The fully divine was incarnated in his person.

The second point arises out of the first. If Jesus is fully divine, how is he related to the divine God and the divine Holy Spirit? The answer follows the dual nature of Jesus, which besides the human, Jesus is divine. This divine nature appears to make God and Jesus two divinities, but not really; since Jesus is the issue of God. Jesus in essence is no different from God, but just the same. The Holy Spirit is the expression of God in the world, and is also full divinity just the same as God. Thus, there are three persons, Father, Son, and Holy Spirit, each fully the same divinity, but in three persons. This is the doctrine of the Trinity.

The worship services of Christianity are similar in all the branches. They include praises, hymns, scriptures, liturgical admonitions, sermons, offerings, and rites of passage. In some churches the praise and prayer parts are read from prepared publications; in other churches they are spoken spontaneously. The leaders go by many titles, a few of them are: apostle, deacon, elder, presbyter, priest, vicar, bishop, archbishop, cardinal, pope, patriarch, evangelist, minister, pastor, preacher, and reverend.

Three rituals are universal in Christianity. The first is a creedal affirmation. In some fashion of words the candidate for membership must acknowledge Jesus as Christ, the son of God.

The second ritual is baptism. Baptism in water by immersion, preferably in running water, was the earliest form. Immersion symbolized burial to the ways of the world and rising to live in the Way of Jesus. Some branches of Christianity now sprinkle or pour water on the head of a candidate instead of administering immersion. By whatever form, baptism confirms a person as a Christian.

The third ritual is Communion. It is a rite of continuing allegiance to Christianity. It is a reenactment of the primal event of the Last Supper Jesus had with his close disciples. At that Last Supper Jesus is said to have broken bread at the table and told the disciples that it was his body being broken for them. Then he passed around a cup of the fruit of the vine and told the disciples that it was his blood being given for the forgiveness of human sins. On the day after the Last Supper, Jesus was executed by crucifixion. Communion commemorates the crucifixion death of Jesus, with the added meaning that his execution was required by God in order to forgive human sin that offended God; thus, it is called Holy Communion. In some churches, Communion is called the Eucharist, meaning thanksgiving for the sacrificial offering Jesus made of himself. Communion also is called in some churches the Last Supper, or the Lord's Supper.

Christianity observes two major festivals, Christmas and Easter. Christmas is a celebration of the birth of Jesus. The date for the birth of Jesus is not known, but the near-darkest day of the year has been chosen to teach that Jesus came to bring light back into the world. Christmas is universally observed on December 25, although some Christians extend the celebration into early January. God's gift of Jesus inspires Christians to give gifts to each other. Pageants, displays of lights, and evergreen trees are later additions to the festival.

Easter is a celebration of the resurrection of Jesus. The date of Easter is calculated by the moon's movement, in the months of March or April. Easter is celebrated with special worship services, pageants, offerings, parades, and festivities.

Christianity today counts its total membership at approximately two billion, three hundred million. The Roman Catholic branch has about one billion, three hundred million. The Coptic Orthodox branch has about seventy million. The Eastern Orthodox branch has about four hundred million. The Protestant Reformation branch has about five hundred million. The Anglican branch has about eighty million.

The sacred scripture of Christianity is the *New Testament*. When it is attached to the *Old Testament*, which is the Christian designation for Judaism's *Tanakh*, it is called the *Bible*.

In the twentieth century, the Ecumenical Movement was begun to reunite all the branches of Christianity. The Movement has formed an organization of its own, headquartered in Geneva, Switzerland, with the title of World Council of Churches. Although the Movement has not reunited Christianity organizationally, it has brought about fellowship among the groups. The Council also conducts cooperative endeavors of relief and service throughout the world.

Christianity is a universalizing religion. It evangelizes in hope of converting the world to the Jesus Way. It has endured prosecution and persecution at times. It is often the target of criticism for its beliefs and practices. It is composed of humans who can, but aspire not to, sin. In spite of the untoward times it has experienced in its two thousand years of existence, and in spite of the multitude of common human ills and misfortunes, Christianity promises heavenly eternal afterlife to the members who endure.

10

Islam

Islam teaches that God is the one and only God (Allah) who demands absolute submission to his will and ways, as revealed to the Prophet Muhammad.

The beginning revelation from Allah through his angel messenger, Jabril/Gabriel, was given to Muhammad ibn Abdullah ibn Quraysh (son of Abdullah, tribe of Quraysh) in the early seventh century CE. The year 610 is the commemorative date. Although this date is approximately two thousand, four hundred fifty years after Abraham of Judaism, Islam considers the Abrahamic tradition to be part of its own.

Muhammad (570–632) was the founder and leader of Islam until his death. Muhammad was raised in the city of Mecca. He was buried in the city of Medina/Yathrib. The two cities are on the western coast of the Arabian Peninsula in the modern state of Saudi Arabia.

Muhammad's father died before Muhammad was born. His mother died shortly after Muhammad's birth. Muhammad was raised in the home of his uncle, Abu Bakr/Abdullah ibn Uthman, chief of the Quraysh tribe.

Muhammad was not eligible to attend school because he was an orphan. He began working for a caravansary. He quickly learned the trade. He soon was leading a caravan train operated by a widow, Khadija. Muhammad and Khadija fell in love and married. They had sons and daughters; the youngest daughter, Fatima, grew to maturity and married Ali ibn Abi Talib.

Muhammed had a spiritual side which he nurtured through meditation and prayer. One of his favorite meditation spots was a cool cave at Mount Hira. Especially he thought about the way people lived in Arabia. While the people had blessings, they also had banes, such as idolatry. Each of the said three hundred sixty five tribes on the peninsula had its own god made of earthly materials. Muhammad's tribe, Quraysh, was heavily involved in the image memento business in Mecca as the tribes came to this hub city to shop. Another bane was drunkenness, aggravated by their long trips on caravan routes and/or their idle times in the shade of their tents. Another bane was warfare. The tribes raided each other for supplies and territory. Fighting and even killing others was part of the way of life.

Muhammad meditated long about the conduct of the Arabian peoples. On the night between Ramadan 26–27, 610 CE, he heard the unmistakable words of Allah through angel Jabril telling him to recite messages of judgment and conduct. This night is revered as the Night of Power and Excellence / Night of Destiny. Muhammad was commanded to recite "in the Name of your Lord" from memory what had been revealed to him. He proceeded to do so. Khadija and close friends accepted the messages. Uncle Abu Bakr also believed him. Muhammad accepted the title of Prophet.

Others in Mecca, especially government, economic, and religion factions, ridiculed and condemned him. The city establishment opposed him because they considered their traditional mores to be sacrosanct. When Muhammad began his street preaching it caused such a public stir that the government took quick notice.

The economic faction opposing Muhammad was led by his own tribe, the Quraysh. The Quraysh profited greatly from the religion icon business. The many tribes in Arabia came to Mecca on trading excursions. They bought icons of their tribal gods which were pedaled at the Quraysh-controlled bazaars. Muhammad declared that all the gods other than Allah were false, which made the many tribal religions false. Muhammad's declaration deprived his own tribe of sales and income.

The religion faction opposing Muhammad erupted when Muhammad proclaimed that Allah had commissioned him to recite radical changes in the ways his people lived on the Arabian Peninsula. Not only his recited changes, but also his claim to be the latest and last divinely chosen prophet was deemed too much insolence for an orphan who had led camel caravans. The critics noted that this bodacious latecomer had married a noteworthy widow and had gained access to her wealth.

The opposition to Muhammad became so unbearable that he and his believers fled to Medina. Medina's leaders happened to be in bitter controversy at this moment. They had heard of Prophet Muhammad as being a reliable and fair person. They selected him to be their mayor, as it were, with full authority to weigh and order. He ruled with approval. He recruited an army and did battle on the peninsula with troops from Mecca. He was wounded, but survived.

By 632 CE, Prophet Muhammad through warfare and/or persuasion had brought virtually all of Arabia under his political and religion dictates. His message was for people to submit to Allah as the true one and same God whom the Jewish patriarchs had worshipped, and accept himself as the final and authoritative Prophet of God/Allah. He rejected Judaism on his charge that it revered the *Torah* above God himself. He rejected Christianity on his charge that it divided the one God into three—Father, Son, and Holy Spirit.

After the death of Muhammad, the leadership of Islam was contested between the person elected by the Muslim community, and the closest blood relative of Muhammad. The community chose Abdullah ibn Uthman / Abu Bakr (surrogate parent of Muhammad). He was challenged by the closest blood relative of Muhammad, Ali ibn Abi Talib (son-in-law, husband of Fatima; no male children of Muhammad were surviving). The majority of Muslims followed the community-chosen line of leaders. These Muslims go by the title Sunni. To our day this persuasion of Muslims is the largest, about eighty five percent of the total one billion, six hundred million. The other branch of Muslims is named Shi'a.

Both branches follow the Five Pillars of Faith that prescribe the Islamic way of life. The Five Pillars of Faith are:

1. Shahada—the confession of faith: "I believe there is no god but Allah, and Muhammad is his Prophet."
2. Salat—prayer five times a day, by kneeling, forehead lowered to the ground.
3. Zakat—alms for the needy, school, charity; 2.5 percent of wealth.
4. Sawm—fasting, not eating, drinking, smoking, or engaging in sexual intercourse during daylight hours; fasting is good at anytime, but required during the pilgrimage month of Ramadan.
5. Hajj—at least once in a lifetime pilgrimage to Mecca.

Muhammad's followers gathered the many revelations given to him by Allah. The recitations were recorded and entitled *Qur'an*, which became the sacred scripture of the religion. The passages of the *Qur'an* were organized into one hundred fourteen surahs/chapters. The whole work is rather slim, compared to the many volumes of interpretation later written on it. Some of the passages refer to the patriarchs of Judaism; some refer to Jesus and his mother, Mary. Prophet Muhammad taught that the *Qur'an* is the eternal, uncreated, literal word of Allah, written in the divine language of Arabic. Later leaders advised that if the *Qur'an* is to be understood correctly it must be read in Arabic.

Islam combined both state and religion for many centuries. The Sunni branch adopted a leadership called caliph. The major ecumenical caliphates for the Sunni in the Near East were:

- Rashidun Caliphate, Arabia (632–661).
- Umayyad Caliphate, Damascus (661–750).
- Abbasid Caliphate, Baghdad (750–1258).
- Abbasid Dynasty/Caliphs, Cairo (1258–1517).
- Ottoman Caliphate, Turkey (1517–1924).

The Shi'a called their leaders imams. They won a large following in Morocco, Egypt, Syria, Iraq, and Persia/Iran.

A third group of Muslims, the Sufi/Tasawwuf, overlaps the two main groups. Sufis are the spiritualistic Muslims who seek a deeper union with Allah than the common members show. Sufis add concentrated meditation and asceticism to Islam. Some dance in a hallucinatory manner. The Sufi goal is to unite with Allah so completely that they and Allah work alike in the world. Sufis are not counted as a third sect of the religion, but a way of experiencing Allah more fully. Sufism is voluntary. Both Sunnis and Shi'as may participate in Sufism.

Islam has a variety of opinions within it on religion matters. The opinions range from very strict to nonparticipating, as do all the other ten religions in our study. Directions for members are stated in two places, the *Qur'an* and the *Hadith*. The *Hadith* is a collection of homely ways of Muhammad, almost as sacred as the *Qur'an*, on personal conduct, such as:

- Do not create any likeness of Allah.
- Do not be unkind to parents.
- Do not kill your children for fear of poverty.
- Do not do shameful deeds.
- Do not harm your soul.
- Do not touch an orphan's property.
- Do not conduct business dishonestly.
- Do not lie.
- Do not break your promises to Allah.
- Do not get off Allah's straight path.

Today Islam has no central authority. Schools of interpretation are several, such as Hanafi, Maliki, Shari, and Hanbali in Sunni Islam. A notable modern movement in Sunni is the Wahhabis located mainly in Saudi Arabia. Some of the schools of interpretation in Shi'a are the Seveners, Twelvers/Ja'fari, Zaidi, and others. The primacy of religion beliefs over secular ways is called Shari/Shariah Law. Titles of leaders of Islam, beside caliph and imam, are ayatollah, emir, mufti, mujtahid, mullah, and shaikh.

The sovereignty of Allah has been a lively topic for Muslim scholars from various schools. The general teaching is that Allah is in total control of history. Allah therefore has foreknowledge of all happenings, past, present, and future. This foreknowledge power includes what moral choices humans will make, but it does not control those choices. Humans are responsible for their moral choices. Allah will judge whether human moral choices/actions are good or evil at the end of time on resurrection day. Allah will judge as carefully as the sharp edge of a sword. Allah will pronounce whether persons have acted good enough to enter eternal divine paradise, or not good enough and be sent to hell.

The matter of diet has been settled with very much the same dos and don'ts as in Judaism. The right way is called halal. The wrong way is called haram.

The place of women was a concern of Muhammad. Before his coming, women were treated as property on the Peninsula, subject to strict male domination. Female infanticide was not uncommon; Muhammad forbade this. He limited the number of wives permitted to a man to four, but to only one unless all were treated equally. He revised divorce laws to give divorcees property rights, and the right to initiate divorce in certain circumstances. He admonished women to dress modestly, but he did not prescribe further modes of face or head coverings that some women practice today.

Mecca is the center of loyalty for all branches of Islam. Mecca is the site of the Kaaba, the structure erected over the rock where Abraham allegedly attempted to sacrifice his son to prove his loyalty to God—note that the son herein is Ishmael, not Isaac as in Judaism. Mecca is the locale of the Great Mosque of Mecca / Al-Masjid al-Ḥarām / The Sacred Mosque. Mecca is the destination of millions of Muslim pilgrims during the month of Ramadan. Access to Mecca is limited to adherents of Islam. Part of this pilgrimage includes Medina, where Muhammad is buried.

Islam celebrates several festivals, notably Hijra / New Year in the month of Muharram (August), Eid al-Fitr / Fast Breaking return to normal life after Ramadan in Shawwal (June), Eid al-Adha/ Sacrifice month of pilgrimage and Abraham's sacrifice (August), and Mawlid an-Nabi (November) birthday of Muhammad. The calendar for Islam starts in the year of the Hijra to Medina, in the common calendar year of 622 CE. Islam begins numbering that as the year 1 AH.

Islam is a universalizing religion. It has a historic drive to convert the world to the way revealed to Muhammad. It has spread throughout the world. Conversion to Islam is simple: recite with utmost sincerity the first Pillar of Faith, the Shahada, three times. Then, members must follow the *Qur'an* and the ways of Prophet Muhammad.

Muhammad clearly taught the hardest battle to fight is not with armaments trained on an external enemy, but with a person's own struggle to live virtuously. Those members who submit to Allah can endure any of Earth's ills, pass through the Day of Judgment with approval, and enter eternal Paradise.

11

Baha'i

BAHA'I PROPOSES TO ESTABLISH a universal religion that enables persons to endure life on Earth and then be reunited with God eternally.

Baha'i was announced in 1863 CE. That date is only something over a hundred years ago, an extremely short time when measured against the hundreds or thousands of years of the other ten religions of our study. Baha'i, however, traces its progenitors all the way back to Abraham of Judaism, about three thousand, seven hundred years ago. Baha'i arose out of an immediate background of Shi'a Islam in a country which opposed Baha'i and tried to eliminate it: Iran.

Baha'i was predicted by a predecessor in 1844 CE. The announcer of the coming of Baha'i was named Siyyid Alí Muhammad Shírází. He went by the title of Bab (the Gate). He lived in Persia/Iran. He was a Shi'ite Muslim. The Shi'ites sought the leadership of all Islam at the death of Muhammad, but they were not chosen. Consequently, they started their own line of leaders. Twelve men held the leadership down to the ninth century. The twelfth successor one day just disappeared. Shi'ites believed he would reappear in the world someday.

Siyyid claimed a divine revelation had come to him that he was the twelfth Imam who had disappeared nine hundred years earlier. He began teaching the revelation that a universal religion based on truth was possible. He began outlining a series of social and religion reforms as the start toward a universal religion. The reforms were so radical in the opinion of the Shi'a establishment that they arrested him and eliminated him with a firing squad in 1850. Just before being shot to death, he predicted a messiah would come soon to complete the work he was beginning.

One of Siyyid's followers took up the messianic role. In 1863 Husayn ibn Ali announced the revelation that he was the person Siyyid had predicted. He, too, was condemned by the Shi'a establishment. Husayn was from a wealthy family with political influence, and so was not executed; however, he was exiled by the Iranian regime. Husayn had no home in his own country from 1863 to his death in 1892. Exile did give him chance to spread his message. Toward the end of his exile he was under mere house arrest, which gave him opportunity to write volumes about the new universal religion. One of his works became the sacred scriptures for Baha'i, the *Kitab-i-Aqdas*.

Husayn was a charismatic person who made disciples wherever he went. He accepted their adoration under the title of Baha'u'llah, which translates to "the glory of God." He called his followers Baha'is.

The teachings of Baha'u'llah Husayn are revolutionary to orthodox Shi'a tenets. The universal religion he proclaimed would be marked by truth from all sources, be they religions, sacred scriptures, science, scholarship, cultures, reason—any source whatsoever. Humans would live by the truth which would bring peace, happiness, and endurance beyond all ills of life. He taught that the *Qur'an* is to be read in many passages symbolically rather than literally. Also symbolic are heaven and hell; heaven is closeness to God, hell is distance from God. Angels and evil spirits/jinnis are imaginary, unreal. He taught that literal interpretations of the many myths in the other three Near East religions shackle the human pursuit of meaning and destiny.

Baha'u'llah Husayn insisted that all religions come from the same source, God. The sacred scriptures of all religions are to be respected. The scriptures are not closed; further revelation can and does take place. Revelation is progressive, it brings further truth. Other messiahs will appear in the future.

The key teachings of Baha'i are the oneness of humanity, in one world, under one God. All cultures, all nationalities, all religions, all sexes, all humanity are one at base.

From the sacred scriptures of Baha'u'llah Husayn come these principles:

- All religions teach the same essentials and ought to be unified.
- Truth should be sought unhindered by tradition or superstition.
- Science and religion supplement each other.
- There is equality of men and women.
- Compulsory education is a must.
- Universal language should be composed.
- Extremes of poverty and wealth should be abolished.
- World council of nations should be formed.
- Service to others is as commendable as worship.
- Justice must prevail worldwide.
- Peace is the supreme meaning of life.
- Make pilgrimages to the holy sites.
- Fast especially nineteen days in March to bring in the New Year.
- Pray to express trust in God.

Baha'u'llah Husayn added another teaching about evil: there is no such thing as an evil devil who talks to, or tempts people, or angers God. Since God is one and good, evil has not and cannot exist. What humans think is evil is simply the absence of good.

Baha'i has other teachings about conduct. Divorce is permitted only in extreme incompatibility. Divorcees must care for any children they have, especially educationally. Marriage ceremonies may be held amid the extensive gardens of the temple sites, but not in the temples. Worship in the home is encouraged, as well as in a central building. There is no ordained clergy; members of the congregations lead all portions of a meeting. Members support all phases of the religion; offerings may not be received from nonmembers. Alcohol is forbidden. Gambling is forbidden. Narcotics are forbidden.

The teaching about human nature is that it is good. Humans have the capacity for choosing good conduct. Bases for choosing right living are: (1) unity—accept all revelations as partial messages from God; (2) reason—work in conjunction with the latest findings of all the sciences; (3) peace—strive for a peaceful world order, all national boundaries are artificial; and (4) equality—equal opportunity, human rights, justice for all.

Baha'u'llah Husayn taught at death a person's body and soul are separated. The body is buried and decays. The soul continues to exist and make its way toward uniting with God. What happens further in afterlife is a mystery.

After Baha'u'llah Husayn's death in 1892 the leadership of Baha'i remained in his family until 1963. In that year the leadership became elected. At the local level, a nine-member Board is elected yearly. At the national level, a nine-member National Spiritual Assembly is elected yearly. At the world level, a nine-member body called the Universal House of Justice is elected from the Baha'i National Spiritual Assemblies every five years. The constant use of the number nine was declared as the most perfect number because it has in it all the other numbers and it is the highest single number.

Baha'i has no ordained clergy/preachers, thus no sermons. Services consist mainly of readings from the sacred scriptures of the major religions, or from writings of Baha'u'llah Husayn.

Baha'is have erected seven temples in the world. Each is an elaborately designed nine-sided structure. The temples serve as administrative centers, worship sanctuaries, and also as tourist attractions because of their unique architecture. The temple in the United States of America is in the suburban Chicago city of Wilmette, Illinois.

Baha'is observe several festivals. Three principal ones are Naw Ruzl / New Year on March 21, the birthday of the Baha'u'llah on November 12, and Ridvan between April 21 and May 2. Ridvan celebrates the date Husayn announced in 1863 that he was bringing the new universal religion of Baha'i.

Pilgrimage sites are several, primarily the Ridvan Garden near Baghdad, Iraq, where Husayn made his founding announcement. Other pilgrimages are made to his burial site in Acre, Israel, and Siyyid's burial site at Mount Carmel, Israel.

The number of Baha'is in the world is about seven million. There are chapters in two hundred eighteen countries. The headquarters of Baha'i are in Haifa, Israel.

Like its parent religion, Baha'i is a universalizing religion. It is missionary-minded and would have all Earth's population convert to Baha'i. Baha'i' has rapidly expanded in less than two hundred years.

Baha'i has not let the beginning evils of firing squad, forced exile, opposition, or discrimination hinder it. Baha'i has suffered bad times, and yet evolves as the religion of choice by millions to enable them to endure life on planet Earth until reason, truth, and peace shall reign.

Note to Readers

THE DESCRIPTIONS OF THE eleven great religions of the world today are based on my class lectures from nearly a half-century of teaching, stripped down to the bare essentials. For your further reading on these religions I suggest you start with the primary materials (sacred scriptures) rather than secondary materials (commentaries and annotations) that pass through the authors' purviews. In reading sacred scriptures you will have a chance to get the feeling of awe that the members of the religions get.

When you read the scriptures do so quickly the first time, in paragraphs or whole units, such as chapters or parts. On a second time, read the scriptures as whole books. Avoid laboring over single words or phrases.

Be aware that all of these religions have volumes upon volumes of literature. For example, the Hindu *Vedas* run into the scores; so pick a few to get the flavor. On the other hand, the *Tao Te Ching* consists of one thin volume even though Taoist writings are countless. If you cannot locate the works listed below for the religions, find a copy of their scriptures online, on YouTube, or in a library.

Primary Materials

Sacred Scriptures,
in Order of the Contents of This Book

THERE ARE MANY PUBLISHED translations and versions of the sacred scriptures of the religions. If you cannot locate these, then select any reliable work of the actual texts—avoiding interjected notes and comments.

Hinduism—Chandrasekharendra Saraswati, trans. *The Vedas.* 7th ed. Mumbai: Sudakshina Trust, 2006.

Jainism—Hermann Georg Jacobi, trans. *Jain Sutras.* Parts 1 & 2. Oxford: Clarendon, 1884.

Buddhism—Yehan Numato, ed. *The Teaching of Buddha: The Buddhist Bible.* Tokyo: Society for the Promotion of Buddhism, 1966.

Sikhism—Ernest Trumpp, trans. *The Di Granth; or, The Holy Scriptures of the Sikhs.* Hong Kong: Forgotten Books, 2018.

Taoism—Stephen Mitchell, trans. *Tao Te Ching.* New York: Harper Perennial Modern Classics, 2006.

Confucianism—Arthur Waley, trans. *The Analects of Confucius.* New York: Random House, 1989.

Shintoism—W. G. Aston, trans. *Nihongi: Chronicles of Japan from the Earliest Times to A.D. 697.* London: Japan Society, 1896.

—O No Yasumaro. *The Kojiki: An Account of Ancient Matters.* Translated by Gustav Helot. New York: Columbia University Press, 2014.

Judaism—Jewish Publication Society. *Tanakh: The Holy Scriptures.* Philadelphia, 1985.

Christianity—National Council of Churches. *The New Testament.* New Revised Standard Version. Nashville: Cokesbury, 1990.

Islam—Talal Itani, ed. *Quran.* English translation. Plano, TX: ClearQuran, 2015.

Baha'i—Moojan Momen. *The Baha'i Faith: A Short Introduction.* Oxford: Oneworld, 1997.

Secondary Materials

THERE ARE MANY BOOKS by many authors on the religions. Here is a brief, selected list. The latest editions have updates, but any edition is good reading.

Bowker, John, ed. *The Oxford Dictionary of World Religions*. New York: Oxford University Press, 1997.

Brodd, Jeffrey, et al. *Introduction to World Religions*. 3rd ed. New York: Oxford University Press, 2015. 1st ed., 1999.

Fisher, Mary Pat, and Robin Rinehart. *Living Religions*. 9th ed. London: Pearson, 2014. 1st ed., 1990.

Hopfe, Lewis M., et al. *Religions of the World*. 13th ed. London: Pearson, 2014. 1st ed., 1983.

La Spina, F. C., ed. *Religions of the World*: *Expressions of Faith and Pathways to the Divine*. 2nd ed. San Diego: Cognella, 2016. 1st ed., 2013.

Noss, David S., and John B. Noss. *A History of World Religions*. 14th ed. New York: Macmillan, 1993. 1st ed., 1949.

Oxtoby, Willard G., et al. *A Concise Introduction to Religions*. 3rd ed. 2 vols. New York: Oxford University Press, 2015. 1st ed., 2008.

Smith, Huston. *The World's Religions*. New York: Harper, 1958. Republished as *The Religions of Man*. New York: HarperCollins, 1965.

Zalta, Edward N., ed. *The Stanford Encyclopedia of Philosophy*. Stanford: Metaphysics Research Lab, Center for the Study of Language and Information, Stanford University, 2020.

www.ingramcontent.com/pod-product-compliance
Lightning Source LLC
Chambersburg PA
CBHW071105090426
42737CB00013B/2490